Thankful for
THE FIGHT

Ready for a rollercoaster ride?

This book will make you laugh and ugly cry, maybe even snort. It's a book of life - real life! Not that "how to lose a guy in ten days" pretend life stuff. No, this book is real. You will read it feeling like you took a real life journey and be thankful you did.

The title of the book was set in stone a year before the idea of a book really came to fruition. I'm an avid blogger (I think that's a thing), and as I would blog about my son's journey through cancer treatment I would always put "Thankful for the fight" in my signature.

No, I'm not thankful my son got cancer, but I am thankful he got to fight it. Growing up, I watched people around me receive calls that their child was gone. No chance to fight - just gone. That was not my experience. We were told our son Cannon had a 50/50 chance of survival. I took that and ran and I am thankful we got to fight! Many parents wish they had that luxury and the hope is that this book illustrates my awareness of that.

All proceeds of this book go to Cannonball Kids' cancer, a children's cancer research foundation started in June of 2014. We are dedicated to finding cures for all childhood cancers by funding critical research needed to improve antiquated treatments and eliminate the occurrence of life-threatening side effects and secondary cancers.

April 26th 2013

8 DAYS

SINCE DIAGNOSIS

Cancer is the number one killer of
children under the age of fifteen.

*Source: Parents Against Childhood Cancer

Don't Take For Granted One Second With Your Child
Written Apr 26, 2013 5:51am

Cannon had a better night than the night before. He is in pain, of course, because they opened him again yesterday, but he is not vomiting and that is great news. Cannon's surgery yesterday to clear an obstruction in his intestines meant we couldn't start chemo yesterday. They need to make sure Cannon's organs are working fully or he will not be eligible to start chemo.

For anyone out there who is reading this, I would say don't take for granted one second with your child. I know Michael and I have never done that and now we have wonderful memories of playing with our boy and a hundred videos of the same. Finding out your child has cancer is the worst news in world, but Michael and I have strong faith in the power of prayer. We don't want our boy to be a statistic. We want him to be a superhero, and he already is in our hearts. I have only been a mumma for twenty months, but my love for this boy lying beside me is like Buzz Lightyear – "To infinity and beyond!" If I could take his place, I would.

" ...tell your kids how special they are and love on them! "

Today, please tell your kids how special they are and love on them! Kids are the best part of this world. Their smiles and naïve natures make our adult lives worth living!

Cannon is my world and has been since he was placed in my arms on August 10, 2011. Next week, Cannon will have twin brothers. Please pray for him to fight this awful disease. I will need his help in keeping these twins in line.

Thanks for all who support our son! Please pray for his beautiful big sister, Olivia, who has a strength like no young woman I've ever known!

Chemo - Arnold Palmer Hospital For Children -- Orlando, Florida
Written Apr 26, 2013 3:31pm

The nurses are in the room giving Cannon his first day of chemo! It's hard to wrap my head around the fact our son is receiving chemo when last week we went to the park, the mall, and swimming with Dad at the YMCA! It's been the craziest week of our lives and, for Michael and me, the hardest! I am only a mum of twenty months but I have never experienced a greater pain! Never! My heart aches for Cannon. Thinking what he is enduring is mental and physical torture!

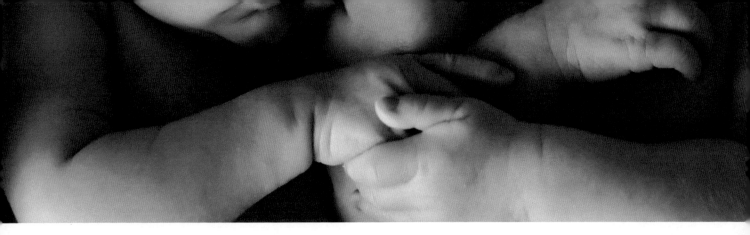

Blood - Twins
Written Apr 30, 2013 6:35am

Cannon is fast asleep. He looks so beautiful and peaceful. Every night, when I would check on Cannon before I went to sleep, I prayed over him. I used to say, "God, you can do anything to me but never take away my son, always keep him safe." I know He has listened and I know in a few years this whole thing will be a bad dream!

Cannon had a blood transfusion for four hours last night. I want to thank all of you who donate blood. You are literally saving lives, like for our son, Cannon.

Today our kids will double. Olivia and Cannon will have two new brothers later today! I am thankful God has allowed me to be a mother once again! Truly the greatest joy and gift to any woman! I will miss my Cannon as I bring Arran James and Gray into the world, but I know his daddy will be loving and spoiling on him while I am across the street at Winnie Palmer Hospital.

" God, you can do anything to me but never take away my son, always keep him safe."

Twins Have Arrived: Happy Birthday To Our New Baby Boys
Written Apr 30, 2013 1:56pm

Both are doing amazing! Six pounds, six ounces and six pounds, three ounces and no time in the Neonatal Intensive Care Unit (NICU)! They both have black hair like their Mumma! The C-section was a piece-of-cake. Hard to complain when Cannon is going through what he is going through.

Thank you for praying for a safe birth and healthy babies. God heard your prayers and both boys are perfect!!

What an amazing honor to be a mumma of four!! Olivia, Cannon, Arran James and Gray are perfect!

May 4ᵗʰ 2013

16 DAYS

SINCE DIAGNOSIS

More children still die from cancer than
Cystic Fibrosis, congenital birth defects,
asthma, diabetes and AIDS combined.

*Source: Children's Hospital of Philadelphia

Not Getting Home: Fever Is Scary In A cancer Patient
Written May 4, 2013 4:26pm

Cannon spiked a fever. Not good news as this means he will stay at the hospital. They have taken a blood culture to see if he has an infection. If he does, he is in the hospital until the next chemo round.

I am on my way to the hospital with the twins to let Cannon meet his new brothers. On our drive, I saw a family with a little two-year-old boy smiling and laughing and petting a dog. Tears ran uncontrollably down my face. Not because I resent them but because I'm sad the next few years of Cannon's life are going to be filled with hospitals and surgeries and blood transfusions and all the things that no child should endure! I want, like all mothers, for my child to be a child and not have pain and sadness in his life. My heart is broken by what Cannon will face and is currently facing. It is now, at this moment, I have to pull on the strength that God and our community give us and be reminded that my son has the opportunity to fight - some kids don't! That is a gift in itself!! It is now I need to be reminded we have health insurance - some families don't! It is now I need to be reminded I have a support network that is beyond incredible - some families don't! It is now, in this moment, I pray to God for healing for my son so he can pet the dog and play like a regular kid!

Twenty-Four Days
Written May 13, 2013 8:02pm

I can't believe it's been twenty-four days since we were admitted to the hospital for what they thought was a bone infection in Cannon's left femur. Twenty-four days ago, at 9pm, after being in the hospital since 9am, we received a call from our oncologist. He said, "I don't think your son has a bone infection. I think he has neuroblastoma." I said, "What's that?" He said, "It's a tumor." The rest I don't recall. I passed the phone to Michael and I Googled "neuroblastoma" on my phone and up came the dreaded word that no one wants to see - "cancer". I started to not breathe. I felt like an elephant was standing on my chest. I walked out of the room and I couldn't breathe. I was overwhelmed with grief. Michael followed me outside the room, wrapped his arms around me, wiped my tears and said "It will be okay, he will be okay."

" The truth is Cannon had a limp and his pediatrician told me it was nothing."

That night, I kept playing over and over again the words, "I think... your son has neuroblastoma." I prayed his thoughts were wrong. I prayed that Cannon was not stage four, as the prognosis was poor.

The following morning at 8am our oncologist came in and said, "Well, the CT scan appears to show a large tumor in the abdomen as well." I said, "What stage?" He said, "Four." I said, "What's the prognosis?" He said, "Fifty-fifty. It's a very difficult cancer to beat. We have a fight on our hands." Typing this is making me feel sick, but so many people are asking, "How did you know what happened?" I wanted to share this with all of you. It's the least I can do for all the prayers our son is getting daily.

The truth is Cannon had a limp and his pediatrician told me it was nothing; he probably just hurt his leg. When they called later to check in on him, I said his leg seemed worse. He told me to look online for an orthopedic doctor, so I did! We had X-rays taken and then, the following day, an MRI. I guess the lesson here is sometimes parents just know when something is up with their kid and sometimes we know when it's not just a limp. Sometimes we just have to push and not take "No" for an answer! We are our children's only TRUE advocates!! The doctors have a hundred patients - but I have only one Cannon, and Michael and I will fight for him for all our days!

Round Two Of Chemo: Day One
Written May 17, 2013 6:18pm

This morning Cannon was so happy and laughing and playing. It was so painful to know where he was going and what the next ten days were going to look like. I was choked up all morning. I haven't been very good today at staying optimistic. I found myself in tears wishing my child could have a normal 20-month-old life. I found myself dwelling on the fact that he will lose his hearing, have speech issues, possibly lose organs, be impotent and a whole host of other things they made us sign off on. I tried to pull myself out of the hole but really didn't do a good job. Tonight I will pray to do better and be stronger. Cannon needs and deserves that, as do Olivia, Michael and the twins.

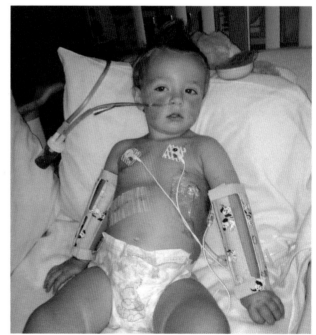

Cannon will have five days of chemo, one day of fluids, and then we are off to Shands Hospital in Gainesville for the stem cell transplant consultation.

God Speaks Through Others
Written May 18, 2013 8:12pm

I mentioned yesterday I would pray for strength to do better for my family. Well, that came to me today in the strangest and most beautiful way possible...

Cannon took a nap so I went to the hospital family room with a magazine to take a break. This young 15-year-old cancer patient came in and sat down beside me. He was frail and had many drips going in him. He smiled at me and said, "Hey." I smiled back and said, "Hi." We started to talk. He was so wise, way beyond his years. The thing I love about children is they say what they think and they are honest beyond what we are capable of as adults. He told me how he was going to be a pediatric oncologist when he grew up and how when he got his wish from the charity Make-A-Wish, he would ask for them to help with paying for medical school since his family couldn't afford it. He has bone cancer and he told me he was lucky they caught it in time. His attitude just made me smile inside. I didn't feel sorry for him, I felt proud. He was beautiful inside and out. I wanted to high-five him, not cry for him!

" He told me how he was going to be a pediatric oncologist when he grew up ..."

We spoke about Cannon and he asked me, "How are you doing?" I said, "I am being strong for my son." And, there it was... God speaking to me in his simple response. He said, "Good, because I can tell you, as a cancer patient, watching your parents in pain and upset is harder than fighting cancer." He said, "Stay strong for him. He needs that more than anything."

So there I was being told by a 15-year-old who has severe bone cancer that he was one of the lucky ones and that I need to stay strong. I don't think for the rest of my days I will forget that conversation.

Our conversation ended with my telling him someday I will look for his name as a pediatric oncologist. I marvel at the kids on this ward! I don't feel sorry for them, I embrace their bravery and courage and I'm i awe of them.

A Quote From My Scottish Pal
Written May 27, 2013 8:29am

Below is a quote I was sent last night by my friend Jackie Bergen, a fellow Scot who lives in Orlando. It's beautiful and so true, and I wanted to share it with you all:

"Cancer is limited... It cannot cripple love. It cannot shatter hope. It cannot corrode faith. It cannot eat away peace. It cannot destroy confidence. It cannot kill friendship. It cannot shut out memories. It canno: silence courage. It cannot invade the soul. It cannot reduce eternal life. It cannot quench the spirit. It cannot lessen the power of the Resurrection." ~Author Unknown

This is truly how I feel. Cancer cannot take away my love for Cannon, my memories of belly laughter, of swimming in the pool, of hugging him in bed. It does not take away my faith in Cannon or my hope that he can beat this. I don't believe Cannon's soul or mine is broken; in fact, it's stronger than ever, as is our courage to fight this awful disease.

As I lie cuddling my baby in bed and he has tears running down his face because of the pain that riddles his body, I think of that quote and I think, "We will beat this Cannon. Mum and Dad have your back, Cannonball!!!!! No one is taking you from me, baby boy! No one!!! Not even cancer!!"

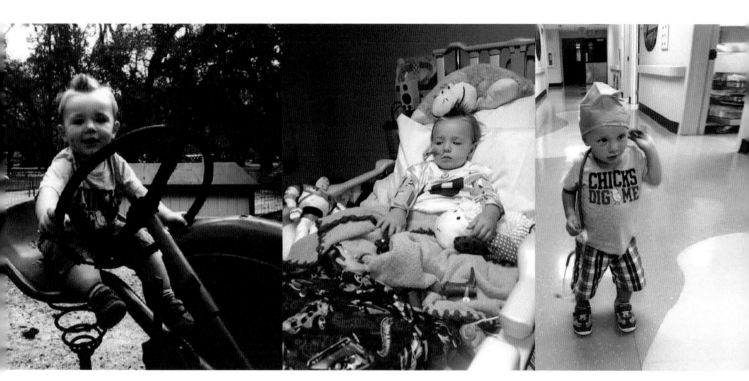

Hospital
Written May 28, 2013 12:11pm

Cannon had a rough day yesterday and was up all night last night. Michael slept in his room with him and I stayed downstairs with the monitor in case either of us fell asleep.

Cannon was so weak today we brought him to the hospital. We knew he needed blood and platelets. He was as white as a ghost and could barely keep his eyes open.

On the drive here this morning, I ended up shaking his legs because his eyes were closed and he was so white I wanted to make sure he was breathing. Of course he was, but I was so freaked out.

" …his eyes were closed and he was so white I wanted to make sure he was breathing."

This morning, Michael was very upset. It's very rough seeing your husband and baby upset and being completely helpless to the situation! Being helpless and out of control are not feelings I deal well with; I am that organized, almost anal (some would say anal :)), person who has schedules on the fridge, hates being late and puts babies' and Mum's clothes out the night before. Yes, the night before! So being out of control and feeling helpless is hard and definitely a huge adjustment for this mum! I just want to make them better and stop their tears.

Cannon is having his blood and platelet transfusions now and this should really help him! His levels were all so low! He is starting to spike a fever so we probably won't get out until we go to Shands, which is looking like Friday now.

When Cannon was diagnosed and we were given the prognosis, I thought, "I don't want the last two years of my son's life in the hospital. I want him to enjoy them." It was a passing thought of fear, but I thought it all the same. Seeing him so weak and so pale is an alarming realization of how sick my son really is and how much he so needs the help of this grueling two year Children's Oncology Group (COG) cancer treatment regime. Some would ask how can I not realize my son is sick? It's not that I don't realize it; it's just that when Cannon is home and happy, I block it out and I embrace and live in the moment with his smiles. That is why it is a punch in the stomach when we see him like he is today.

Every Day Is A Gift - Blog By Dad, Michael Wiggins
Written May 29, 2013 7:37pm

I have a client who lives in the Philadelphia area who for years has always responded to my greeting of, "Steve, how are you?" with the same answer, every time, for as long as I have known him. He says, "Every day is a gift." Several years ago, I spent a lot of time with this gentleman on a series of cases in Florida. Before and since that time, I have seen him at various meetings all over the country, and his response is always the same, "Every day is a gift." I never knew why he said it; I never asked. Now I know it doesn't matter. It's just the flat truth.

Cannon was so ill yesterday. Hard to see. Harder for him. It will get harder, and he will be even sicker. But he will make it. I believe in him and I have told many that someday, Melissa and I will take him on our travels and hold him up as a testament to the power of prayer.

"Every day is a gift."

In Recovery - Stem Cell Collection, Shands Hospital – Gainesville, Florida
Written May 31, 2013 11:11am

You picked the wrong kid to pick on, neuroblastoma. I don't think you realized our baby boy is half-Scottish, half-American - a fierce mix. Just ask Donald Trump!! Although Cannon clearly has better hair!

Cannon is out of the procedure and we are in recovery. Remember, I don't cry in front of Cannon, so I had a little weep before I went in (shhh). Michael is still trying to teach me that crying is not a sign of weakness. I'm working on it but this Scottish woman is hard-headed. Just ask my husband. Cannon is so fierce he is trying to rip the Broviac out of his neck. I am holding his arm to stop him. He is allowed a drink now and he is so thankful for it!

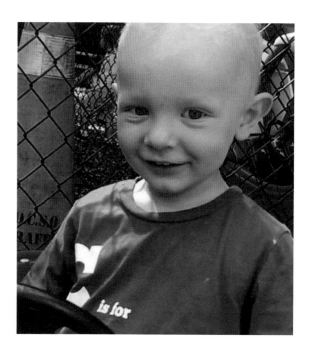

A Record - Stem Cell Collection, Shands Hospital – Gainesville, Florida
Written May 31, 2013 6:19pm

The goal was to get ten million stem cells from Cannon over a three day period (if required). For background information, the head stem cell transplant doctor here at Shands said that the most she has collected is 126 million. Our team in Orlando said the most they have ever collected is 128 million. I told the team here "Let's get 129 million, just for fun", and we all laughed.

Well, isn't my son the little show off?! Most kids at this age are showing off about drawing or running or swimming, but my son is a show off at stem cell production: 155 million! That's right, not 15 but 155 million!!! Dad and I are so proud of our Cannonball. In terms of sport, that's one to Cannonball and zero to neuroblastoma (Dad and I are both sports mad).

Let's hope this is a sign of many things to come...

As I said before, neuroblastoma picked the wrong kid to bully!!!!!

June 8th 2013

51 DAYS

SINCE DIAGNOSIS

Every year, 263,000 new cases of cancer
affect children under twenty worldwide...
that's 720 new cases daily worldwide...
250 children will die TODAY.

*Source: Alex's Lemonade Stand

A Post From Olivia, Our 16-Year-Old Daughter
Written Jun 8, 2013 10:53am

This is Olivia. I am about to leave for a five week summer camp for which I am very excited. What I am not excited for is to leave Cannon. This morning, saying goodbye was one of the hardest things ever. I always knew Cannon's condition was serious but some situations just make everything so much more real. While I'm gone, Cannon will be going through his third round of chemo, which I know is one of the worst. This morning before I left, I took Cannon around the hallways for a quick walk. I stood behind him and pushed his fluids behind as he walked. It makes me sad to see him hooked up to all of the machines and be restrained by all the cords. Despite all of this, he was so happy to be out. I love seeing him smile. Cannon is one tough kid and he has a strong fighting factor in him. Without a shadow of a doubt, I know he will get through this. His strength is so encouraging and I am so, so, so proud of him. He's not only my brother, he is my best friend. He is so important to me and I can't even begin to imagine life without my partner in crime. ;) So, today, please say a prayer the third round of chemo goes well. Thank you for all of the love and support, especially from my friends. The encouraging words are appreciated. Thank you for taking time out of your day to read this and pray for my brother. He means far more to me than you know! :)

" He's not only my brother, he is my best friend."

I Will Take Average
Written Jun 8, 2013 3:12pm

There are days when I have to admit positive thinking isn't my first thought - but I guarantee you it's not my last. I allow myself a few moments of negative thoughts and I pull myself right out of it. Cannon's oncologist came back with the results of Cannon's MIBG scan and didn't seem overly enthusiastic about them, but she wasn't negative either.

She said the spot under his arm is gone. The spots on his knees are less bright. The abdominal tumor, which was 9.6 cm by 6.3 cm and wrapped around all his organs and spine, now has a mushy center and is not as large. I asked by what percentage. She said Cannon's tumor is so large it's too hard to tell. But here is the deal, she didn't come into the room and say it's larger and chemo isn't effective, and that is a blessing. And, she didn't come in and say it is the same size, so that is a blessing, too.

Bone marrow showed no sign of nb cells, which they did prior to chemo. However, this doesn't mean it's gone, as they only sample from two points. This makes it hard to be really happy and enjoy the news since neuroblastoma has a fifty-fifty chance of relapse. I am fearful... that is the honest truth.

I asked the oncologist if she was happy and she said, "It's an average response." To those of you who know me, you know I don't do average or half-hearted but, on this occasion, I will take it. I will take average and I will embrace it!!! The results could have been far worse and the fact Cannon is making small improvements is all I need to hear.

For today I will take average. I know not everyone gets that!

Chemo, Round Three - Blog By Dad, Michael Wiggins
Written Jun 9, 2013 6:30am

Our little guy is struggling through his third round of chemotherapy. He has not taken well to either chemo drug, Etoposide or Cisplatin, and has had reactions, bad nausea and a lot of vomiting. It is maddening to watch medical poison be sent through a line into your child, only to know that it will bring about the short-term result of more extreme sickness and misery to him. My gut wrenches tighter every time and my heart sinks for him. He has never hurt a soul and yet has to endure it. Please pray for God to relieve Cannon's suffering in the short-term and for the treatment to do what it is supposed to do, and kill these ungodly cancer cells, so that in the long-term, the misery will be worth the benefit of a lifetime of health, free of cancer, for Cannon.

Tomorrow, Melissa and I will fly to New York to meet with the surgeon at Sloan Kettering. The thought of both of us leaving Cannon behind in such a poor state - unwell and being given more chemo to make him more sick - is, to say the least, a horrible feeling as a parent. But, we do it in hope that the trip up and back will result in a future surgery, which will remove the tumor completely from his body and move us one step closer to Cannon's recovery in full health.

Dr. La Quaglia - Memorial Sloan Kettering Cancer Center -- New York, New York
Written Jun 11, 2013 5:55pm

We are on the plane on the way back to Orlando from New York, so now seems a good time to type an update.

Michael and I are so humbled and thankful we were able to meet with the number one nb surgeon in the country, if not the world – Dr. La Quaglia at Sloan Kettering. We know there are so many families who wish they could have the privilege and, trust me, we do not take it for granted. From the week Cannon was diagnosed we knew this guy was our guy and we would do all in our power to meet with him.

We were prepared with a vast array of questions thanks to research and other families.

My heart hurts as I type this, but, in terms of complexity, Dr. L said, "With one being the least and ten being the most, Cannon is a ten. This is going to be tough and this is a life threatening surgery." Dr. L went on to say the tumor is so complex that one surgery is NOT likely to suffice. This is very unusual, he told us, because in nine out of ten cases he is able to get the tumor out in one go. Cannon will need at least two surgeries lasting between eight and twelve hours. Cannon's case is so bad that even though round one and two of chemo have shrunk the tumor somewhat, it is still so large it encases his kidneys, liver, and all of his organs including his aorta and vena cava. When Dr. L was explaining this to me, I was using every fiber of my being to hold back my tears and act professional because I had a job to do. I had questions to ask as Cannon's advocate. This was not the time or place to cry. I managed to stay strong and ask all my questions, as did my amazing husband. If I haven't mentioned it enough, my husband is amazing and no one more perfect for this Scottish lass from Irvine (proud of it, too). As I say to Michael all the time, "You fit me like a glove." We will celebrate three years of marriage on Sunday.

I asked Dr. L if he thought he could do it and he said he would try. That line is so hard to type. A world-renowned surgeon says he will try. First, I am so thankful he will take on Cannon, but second, if Cannon's tumor is complicated for him, then that's bad news. I am not naïve to that fact. I am pained by it beyond belief, beyond any pain I've experienced. It's physical and emotional. Michael and I knew it was bad but it just seems to get worse and worse.

We also met with Dr. Kushner (the lead oncologist), an amazing man - we both loved him! He went over Cannon's MIBG scan and showed us how bad the metastasis is in his legs. He said he was surprised Cannon's leg had not broken. He spent a significant amount of time educating us. I think he thought he was in a deposition with two lawyers. I feel like I am preparing for the trial of my life - the most important thing in my life - saving my son's life! Michael and I hate to lose and this is a battle we can't, and won't, lose.

After our meeting, I went into the bathroom and I got on my knees and I prayed to God and said, "Please don't take my son, please don't take my son, please don't take my son. I can't live without him! He is my everything!" I don't believe God gave Cannon cancer, but I do believe I get strength from Him, and all who pray, to be Cannon's best advocate and to make him smile everyday - no matter what!! My heart is broken, but I believe when Cannon is cured, he will be healed and so will my heart.

Life After Chemo, Round Three
Written Jun 14, 2013 10:32am

I want to say that I am thankful Cannon is out of the hospital, and I am, but sometimes it's harder out of the hospital. We didn't even get off of the hospital's grounds and Cannon was vomiting all over the car. I was driving, and to watch my baby just vomit over and over again in the mirror and see the pain and confusion on his face felt like how I imagine a knife in my chest would feel. He is a trooper, I'm the weak one. I need to take a page out of his book.

The last two nights, we have spent the wee hours of the morning cleaning up vomit. I sat in the shower with him just letting the water hit on his back as he vomited. I think that helped him a little. He won't eat very much, and when he does it's right back up. This, I'm told, is called delayed nausea - poor baby!

As I have said before, I really believe it's emotionally harder on Michael and me. Last night, after Cannon literally covered me in sickness from head-to-toe, he wanted to play American football and hide-and-seek. The kid amazes me beyond belief... my hero.

Today we did labs. Even though there are twenty-one days between chemo treatments, there are not twenty-one days off. They are filled with outpatient things like scans and bloodwork, oh, and the dreaded fever that becomes inpatient.

Stop!!!!!
Written Jun 14, 2013 11:46pm

I want the vomiting to stop!!!!!

Cannon has endured enough and the delayed nausea is seriously kicking his butt. His ribs and bones are showing and he is losing weight by the day. It's enough - stop!!! He is too weak to play and falls over when he walks as his energy is so low. Third round of chemo is rough.

I ask you all to pray for Cannon to gain strength through your prayers, to not be scared, to eat and to be able to kick this sickness in the butt! He needs strength!

My heart aches. At night, I watch him on the monitor, and three nights in a row I had to run to his room as he was vomiting everywhere. He is an angel and he just wants to sleep. STOP. Let him sleep.

I pray that I can find strength as a mother to keep my tears for my pillow and stay strong for my son - one day at a time.

Happy Father's Day
Written Jun 15, 2013 10:36pm

As I type, my amazing husband is running and jumping on the bed and Cannon is giggling like crazy. It has to be the best sound in the whole world, to hear your kid laugh. It melts my heart. Michael is an unbelievable father and our four kids are so lucky to have him as a dad. He makes them laugh and feeds them bad food... what could be cooler in a father? (I'm the bad guy... LOL). That's ok, I can handle it. But seriously, when I got married I knew Michael was an amazing father, but his strength for Cannon in all

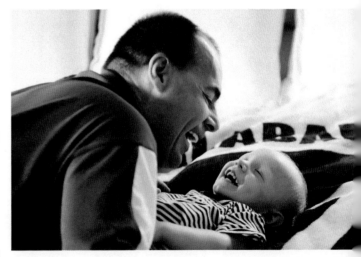

this is amazing to me. He and Cannon are my heroes!! I'm very lucky to have them in my life.

Happy Father's Day, Babe. Happy Father's Day to you all!! Being a father is a gift and one we should never take for granted. Enjoy this special day with your children.

Cannon had the best day since round three of chemo. I'm so thankful for a good day. He is smiling and laughing and eating a little. Answered prayers.

Faith

Written Jun 21, 2013 9:35am

It is no coincidence that when I created the CaringBridge page the week Cannon was diagnosed, I chose the background design "FAITH"...

> *" I have never once asked,*
>
> *'Why Cannon?'*
>
> *I'm sure what will come back is,*
>
> *'Why not?'"*

Where I come from (Scotland), people don't talk about faith or God. It's just not spoken about. I am not saying that is right or wrong, but it's different than the U.S. In the U.S., God and prayer are very much spoken about. I admit, it was an adjustment for me but one I have come to relish and love.

As one could imagine, faith COULD be tested when your 20-month-old is diagnosed with stage four cancer. One could ask, "Why my child? Why cancer?" One could easily lose her faith. I am happy to report I have not. In fact, my faith is stronger than ever. I have never once asked, "Why Cannon?" I'm sure what will come back is, "Why not?" I have not once believed God gave my son cancer. He did not. But, He gave me a lot of things, including faith.

For me personally, faith is not about religion. For me faith is about two things: it's about HOPE and it's about BELIEVING. Anyone of any religion, or of no religion, can have faith.

I now have family members who never prayed before or believed in the power of prayer, praying daily. That's faith and that's believing.

I believe Cannon is being given strength through everyone's prayers.

I have hope that all who pray for Cannon continue to for years to come.

I believe Michael and I will raise lots of money in the future to help families like ours.

I have faith Cannon can beat this evil cancer.

This to me is faith, in which I have an abundance.

Live In The Moment

Written Jun 22, 2013 3:51pm

Yesterday Cannon and I were at the hospital all day. He needed blood and platelets. It's still overwhelming as a mother to think my little baby needs this to survive because his little body is being attacked by a deadly disease. I am taking the advice of a woman, Silvia Vanni, who is close to me and who lost her son Sal from this disease after years of fighting hard. This is what she told me: "Enjoy every moment. Embrace them all. I would do anything to still be fighting, to still be going across the country looking for clinical trial after clinical trial." I keep that in my heart daily. As I cuddled up with Cannon in the chair and he was having blood pumped in him, I squeezed him so tight and I held his tiny, chubby little hands in my hands and I thanked God for that moment, for the blood and for my son still being alive to hold! I didn't think, "Oh, what we could be doing? I wish we could swim or play at the park." Instead I took my friend's advice. I lived in that moment and I made memories with my son. I love you, Cannonball Wiggins - more than life!! I will fight for you and others till the day I die!

Yesterday Cannon had a reaction to the platelets - that's the second time! The oncologist said his reaction is like a panic attack, like impending doom. That's what it felt like as I watched Cannon scream for forty minutes. I have never seen him act the way he did, such fear in his face and eyes, such pain. I was helpless. I had to restrain him in the chair and he fought me. My heart aches as I type this because he looked at me to save him and I couldn't! He was so terrified by what was happening to him he ripped out his port – there was blood everywhere! We had three amazing oncologists and three amazing nurses all in the room trying to get him calmed down! All I can say is it was a horrific forty minutes. He cried a whimpering cry for an hour afterwards. You know the one I mean. One word... brutal!! For any of you who have had the privilege of spending time with Cannon, you know he is an angel, a really good boy, he doesn't have temper tantrums - not the feet and arm kicking kind. So, to watch that yesterday was horrific to say the least.

Cannon Gives - Blog By Dad, Michael Wiggins

Written Jun 25, 2013 11:07am

It is important, I think, for Melissa and me to stay very connected to the mission and goal we have for our family: To keep our children safe, provide a loving home and have them grow up healthy and with faith. Cannon has given us the gift of perspective on life. The diagnosis of neuroblastoma, and our fight against it, has shown us so many things, not the least of which is the love and heart of our families, friends and our community that stretches across the world. Thank you all, again, for that.

Also, it has shown us that we are, as Melissa says, "Thankful for the fight". What does this mean? It mean we have been given a chance to beat neuroblastoma in Cannon, and someday have him cancer-free, and we have every intention of doing it. We will stop at nothing to save him and give him a life of health from the moment he is cancer-free and beyond. But some parents don't get the opportunity we have been given. Unfortunately, we have close friends and family who have lost their children in sudden tragedies. They did not get the chance to fight for their child. We have been given that opportunity, and we see, and know, how fortunate we are. Therefore, we are, "Thankful for the fight".

Tell One Person
Written Jun 29, 2013 11:41am

Let me give a little background...

I had a chat with our oncologist the other day and, well, let's just say neuroblastoma is not your first pick of pediatric cancer if you had a choice. The prognosis is poor and the treatment is grueling. The prognosis has gone from thirty percent, to a forty to fifty percent survival rate in the last five years. However, my point is this: no one knows what neuroblastoma is. I didn't, and I consider myself a relatively intelligent woman. Everyone does, however, know what leukemia is and as a result, the awareness is higher which equals higher prognosis

"No one knows what neuroblastoma is. I didn't, and I consider myself a relatively intelligent woman."

percentages. Would you believe that most leukemia in children now has a ninety percent survival rate? WOW!! I know in my heart that is partly due to parents of kids with leukemia lobbying for their kids. I intend to do this for Cannon and all kids that have neuroblastoma. Let's beat the crap out of nb.

So my favor is this: Can I ask each of you who read this to, this week, tell one person (who doesn't know what neuroblastoma is) about it? For those who aren't sure what nb is I would explain it in layman's terms like this:

Neuroblastoma is known as the baby cancer and more than half of the cases exist in kids under two. It is the most common solid tumor kids' cancer. There are 700 new cases a year in the US and 100 in the UK. High risk nb has a two-year extensive treatment including chemo, bone marrow transplant, surgeries to remove tumors, radiation and immunotherapy. Right now, it is one of the most difficult childhood cancers to beat when high risk. Relapse is very common, to which some say there is no cure. In the last five years, the survival rate has gone from thirty percent, to a forty to fifty percent chance. That means some 400 kids are dying each year in the US from this disease. TOO MANY...

July 6th 2013
79 DAYS
SINCE DIAGNOSIS

Pediatric cancer is grossly underfunded.
Total government spending on cancer
research each year: $603 million to
breast cancer, $315 million to lung cancer
and $208 million to
ALL 12 childhood cancers.

*Source: Children's Hospital of Philadelphia

cancer Changes You... FOREVER
Written Jul 6, 2013 6:08am

Cancer changes you... or should I say when someone you love has cancer, it changes you.

I was the girl who dreamed of marrying a gentleman, a noble man with good morals - I did that.

I was the girl who dreamed of having children - I did that.

I was the girl who dreamed of being a lawyer - I did that.

Three months ago, I would say I was the happiest I'd ever been in my life. I had, and have, a beautiful marriage, a stepdaughter who is the coolest kid, a son who brings more joy to me than anything or anyone in my life and twin baby boys in my tummy. I used to call my mum in Scotland and say "My life is so perfect it scares me", like I was waiting for the penny to drop. My mum was so happy as all she ever wanted, and wants, for her kids is happiness. I enjoyed every minute of that paradise I lived in. Life is now forever changed.

I open my eyes this morning and I'm consumed by cancer. I have tears for cancer. I sit here at 5am feeding my twins with tears streaming down my face. Tears of fear. Tears of pain.

I am mad.
I am sad.
I am angry.

Thankful For The Fight!

Cancer changes you... FOREVER.

I no longer live in that perfect bubble my mum and I spoke of, that blissful place.

I live in reality.

I live in the cancer world. The world where kids die daily from a disease that riddles my son's body.

I wake up, I think about it.
I eat, I think about it.
I sleep, I dream about it.
It's my reality now.

I pray that never changes.
I want to make a difference.

Michael said it yesterday,
Little has changed...
IT MUST!

My family is forever changed.
And so am I.
I know your plan God.
Your will, not mine, be done.

I say in my writings, "Thankful for the fight". There are no four words that are more true today. Cannon is so early in this fight, and his dad and I plan to do as much as we can to save his life. It may not be much medically, but we feed his soul daily with love and laughter and the occasional hash brown. I am thankful to fight every single minute of every day until I die. I will do this for you, Cannon James Roland Wiggins, and others like you.

Cannon Is Being Changed
Written Jul 11, 2013 3:54pm

We remain in the hospital trying to maintain Cannon's pain. As we do, I see Cannon changing. It is painful to write that because I don't want him to change. He stares into space all the time and I wonder if there are angels around him I can't see. I hope so.

Surgery Looms
Written Jul 14, 2013 11:02pm

Tomorrow marks two weeks until we travel to New York for Cannon's surgery. I have anxiety just typing that. I am so scared. I have been since we were told Cannon would have a twelve hour life-threatening surgery. People tell me Cannon will be fine, he has the best surgeon. The reality is, people don't know Cannon will be fine; I don't know Cannon will be fine. I have to sign a piece of paper for my son, who isn't even two, saying I understand this is a life-threatening surgery. I recall having fleeting thoughts of not having Cannon do surgery. What if he didn't make it? What if I could have had longer with him? What if... What if... What if... The reality is, no one knows what Cannon's fate is except the big man upstairs. I can pray, I can hope, I can live in faith. But the reality is there are people who have done all that and still lost their child to this dreaded disease. Do you think people who lost their children didn't pray? They did. Does that mean I won't pray? No... I pray like crazy all day, EVERYDAY. I pray for so many people, over and over who fight this disease. Does it mean I have no faith because I live in fear? I don't believe so. I have a lot of faith, but am I fearful my son could die? YES SIR, I AM. That's honest, that's raw, that's... REALITY. I know many people say they never thought their child could die from this disease. I am not that way. I realize it's a reality. I listened when the doctor told me Cannon has a fifty-fifty chance. I don't believe Cannon is a statistic, I believe he is a FIGHTER, I believe he is the strongest 23-month-old kid I know. But, I also live in reality. I have seen too much now not to. I don't like reality, so I live in today. I live in the moment, I enjoy every smile I get, every pancake he eats, every time he wants a hug, every swim we take. Michael and I will never stop fighting for him. We will never stop doing what's best for him. I will never stop being Cannon's advocate. I write down every medication he takes, every dose, every cream, the times due, the times administered. I know what to ask for when we get to the hospital room. I do all I can. I will continue to FIGHT for you, Cannon Wiggins.

> "*I listened when the doctor told me Cannon has a fifty-fifty chance. I don't believe Cannon is a statistic, I believe he is a Fighter.*"

Thankful

Written Jul 18, 2013 8:52pm

It is with immense gratitude I type this update. Today was a big day for Cannonball, he had his MIBG and his CT scans to see if the chemo is working. As you know, Cannon has a huge tumor encompassing his entire abdomen and tumors in both legs, under his arm, in his lymph nodes and his bone marrow.

PRELIMINARY RESULTS: I want to say that these are preliminary results. We will have all conclusive results next week. But this is what we were told by our amazing oncologist, Dr. Susan Kelly, at Arnold Palmer Hospital for Children. Cannon's right leg tumor was the size of a golf ball – IT IS CLEAR. This means the MIBG is not detecting any active nb cells. In other words, that tumor is DEAD!!!! Cannon: One – nb: Zero. The tumor under Cannon's arm – CLEAR! Cannon: Two – nb: Zero. Cannon's left leg tumor was HUGE. In fact, we were told they can't believe his leg did not break. His left leg is a bit better – I WILL TAKE IT!!! The primary tumor is less active. Cannon: Three – nb: One. The primary tumor in his stomach is also smaller. Cannon: Four – nb: One. What can I say? My son is a LEGEND in his mind and mine.

I am SO thankful. I am thankful because somewhere today in the US someone was told their child's tumors grew larger, or the treatment wasn't working. I am so thankful because we have options. Would I love scans to show no cancer? Absolutely, but I live in reality and I am so thankful for the results we got today.

The Best Exhaustion: Three Weeks Off Before Surgery

Written Jul 24, 2013 3:55pm

I am exhausted. But not the exhausted I have experienced the last three months. There are no beeping machines here, there are no wires hanging from Cannon, no IV pole trailing behind him as he roams the corridor. Instead there is love, laughter, park trips, swimming sessions, YouTube video sessions, soccer lessons (spoiled much?), movie visits, ice cream before bed, snacks all day and Disney trips. Oh yes, I am exhausted, but the best exhausted feeling in the world. Exhausted because we are jam-packed with fun time and family time and above all, NO HOSPITAL time. Ok, well a little, but nothing like what Cannon and our family lived the three weeks prior. I have so much gratitude for this time we are having, for this normal life we are living and I am in love with our life.

Surgery Time - Memorial Sloan Kettering Cancer Center -- New York, New York

Written Jul 30, 2013 9:54am

We are sitting on the plane and en route to New York for the big surgery. This morning Cannon and I played in the pool. He was one happy boy - laughing, giggling, smiling, jumping in, swimming under the slide, throwing toys in and playing with the balls. I have no idea how I will do it when I have twin two-year olds and Cannon in the pool together... one day at a time. Cannon and I had so much fun. It's painful to now be on our way to New York. This angel knows nothing about what's coming. I'm glad! Let him live a fun life as long as this evil cancer will allow!

As we swam I confess a bad thought popped into my head. What if this is the last time we play together in the pool? My heart sank. No, no, Melissa, don't think like that. I prayed in that instant. I asked God to please give me strength to keep positive thoughts in my head and not allow bad thoughts. In that instant I was relieved of that thought and enjoyed our time! Mother and son! Go, Cannonball!

The other day, Michael's friend and law partner, Gary Toole, came to the house and said to Michael, "Bring him back." When I heard those words, it hit me like a truck. What if we don't? How could I ever come home to this house without my baby? Our baby? My most precious gift from God? But then I realized, I have to let the surgeon try. I have to allow him the privilege of working on my son, our son, to save his life. Right now as I type, Cannon is in my arms cuddling me with his blankee and his iPad and cuddled up so cozy! I could stay in this moment forever! I don't want to take him to Sloan Hospital tomorrow. But then I realize, there is no better surgeon, there is no better place to save my son's life. What a privilege and honor to have Dr. L work on Cannon. A gift, an answered prayer for sure. Since the week Cannon was diagnosed, we were in talks with Sloan about Cannon's surgery.

As I come to the end of this journal entry, Cannon sleeps in my arms. I love his smell. Not the baby smell but he has a beautiful baby-like smell. The tears roll down my face as I play my music and zone out the world. It's only Cannon and me! Me and my baby! I love you more than life, Cannon. If I could have the surgery I would, I would do it 100 times for you to not need to fight this fight! A fight no one should fight 23 months old or ever! You're amazing, Cannon. You're the most amazing two-year-old boy I've ever met! You're an angel sent to me from God! I promise you this, Cannon - I will NEVER give up, I will NEVER stop fighting for you and others! NEVER!!

August 1th 2013

105 DAYS

SINCE DIAGNOSIS

Sadly, the American Cancer Society
(ACS) directs only one cent to childhood
cancer research for every dollar of public
support. So for every $1,000 donated
to ACS, $10 goes to kids' cancer. The
Leukemia and Lymphoma Society is not
much better with directing two cents of
every dollar donated.

*Source: St. Baldrick's

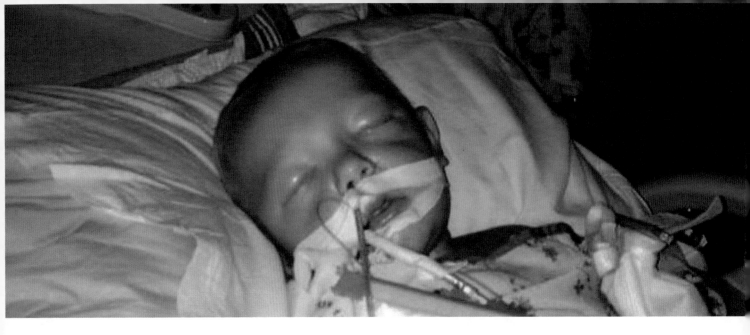

Bring It: The Night Before A Thirteen Hour Tumor Resection Surgery

Written Aug 1, 2013 9:40pm

Bring it, neuroblastoma – we've got you pegged. Bit-by-bit, step-by-step we are going to destroy every last cell in Cannonball's body. You've got nothing on this kid. Though I admit you are a fierce opponent, you've got nothing on our baby boy or his team.

It's the night before the big surgery. I have wondered what I would feel like on this night for many months. Well, this is how I feel: I feel like we are one of the most fortunate families in the entire world. We have THE surgeon - whom many would do anything to have, whom many try to have. A blessing, above all. Thank you, Dr. L. I don't, and won't, take this for granted.

As I sit at a New York Starbucks and watch people go by, I realize nobody knows what people have going on in their lives and maybe I shouldn't judge the lady who doesn't smile back at me, or the man who is grumpy with me in the line for coffee. No one knows what's going on in other peoples' lives and maybe, rather than chastise these people, we should just keep smiling!

As I sit here, what Dr. L said rings in my head... "This surgery is a tough one." It's still a "ten" in terms of complexity, despite the shrinkage of the primary tumor. Dr. L showed us on the scan how he could not possibly get through to the tumor on the left side, so Cannon would need two surgeries. Cannon will have a large incision on his right side to remove that side of the tumor. He will lose his adrenal gland, possibly a kidney, and lymph nodes. He will possibly have a biopsy of the liver and a few other parts. We have to leave for the hospital around 5am tomorrow and Cannon's surgery will be at 7am until around 7pm. So please pray hard for our baby!!!!

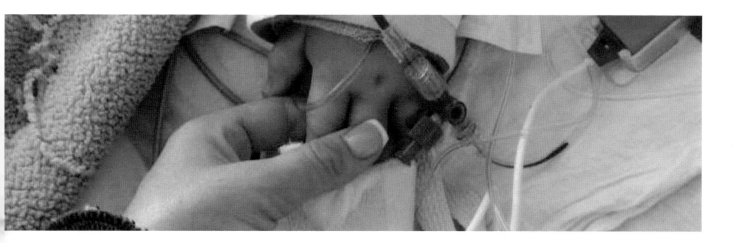

This Is To You, Cannonball:

Everything I do is for you!
I loved you before you were born.
Before I could persuade Dad to have babies. ;)
I wanted a baby for years before you were born,
little did I know you were what I was waiting for.
The day I became pregnant was the happiest of my life.
The next happiest was breastfeeding you in my arms when you were cleaned up (no offense, LOL).
The next was watching you eat food.
The next was watching you crawl.
The next was watching you walk.
The next was watching you and Dad laugh together.
Cannon, every happiest moment of my life is you!!!
You're my happiest moment.
You're my everything.
My first baby.
I love you from my head to my toes.
I never complained to get up with you during night or when you needed to feed every two hours because you were a big boy.
I have loved and love every single second with you.
I thought I was happy before you arrived,
but you're my cherry on top.
You have made me the woman I believe I am.
Loving you is the easiest thing in the world.
Being your mum is the greatest.

I am by your side in the surgery tomorrow, I am right there.
Do not falter, my baby.
Mummy has your back,
for now and forever.
My love for you will never die.
Now listen close,
go kick some serious butt tomorrow.
Don't falter.
Stay strong.
I know you will make Mum so proud.
You have done so every other day of your life (even in timeouts).
I knew you were a special child the day I met you.
But now I know you are an angel sent from God.
We have some serious hard work to do when you beat neuroblastoma.
So pull your bootstraps up,
tuck in your shirt,
and let's do this...

love,

Your ever, ever adoring mum
Mummy Wiggins

P.S. - You rock, Cannonball!

Give Thanks - Surgery Update By Dad, Michael Wiggins

Written Aug 3, 2013 8:19am

Dr. La Quaglia finished just before 9pm last evening, and after almost thirteen hours of surgery, he met with us and told us he believes he removed almost all, if not all, of Cannon's tumor. I wish I could adequately describe for everyone how difficult this was to do, and how amazed and happily astounded Melissa and I are to have heard this news. Dr. La Quaglia told us previously this was a very difficult tumor to remove, we likely could lose a kidney, and because of the tumor's involvement with the aorta and vena cava vessels, there was a possibility Cannon would not survive the surgery. The tumor wrapped around blood vessels to his intestines, and down into his pelvis. Dr. La Quaglia spent an entire day in surgery and believes he has removed it all with no sacrifice of organs, an average loss of blood (he only lost one pint during the whole day, and it was replaced) and of course, Cannon is with us this morning. This is one highly skilled human being, and I am thankful we were guided to find him and to take Cannon to who, we believe, is the finest neuroblastoma tumor resection surgeon in the world.

" I just can't find enough words to explain the gratitude and thanks we have to all of the people who literally prayed for Cannon all day."

As a parent, and a Dad, I just can't find enough words to explain the gratitude and thanks we have to all of the people who literally prayed for Cannon all day. Melissa and I received messages throughout the day, the night before, and still, from throughout the United States, from friends in other countries, and family in Scotland and throughout the UK. I can only relay what Dr. La Quaglia kept saying to us when we continually thanked him late last night. Every time we thanked him for what he did for Cannon, he stepped to the side and pointed upward and said, "Not me."

Cannon is now in the Pediatric Intensive Care Unit (PICU) and will be kept sedated and on a ventilator for a few days to give his body an opportunity to rest. He doesn't look so good, and as a parent it is quite scary to see all the tubes coming from your child who is all swollen and not conscious. We continue to pray because he is not out of danger just yet. We recognize that tumor removal is but one step in the battle to make Cannon cancer-free. We face more chemotherapy, radiation and a stem cell transplant. There is still a road ahead, and while it is not as long as it once was, it will still be difficult. But today, we give thanks: to our family members for their love, support and help; for our friends at home in Florida for the community support; and those all throughout the world who continually lift us up in prayer and offer words of encouragement; and most importantly, to our Lord, who answered my prayers and showered Dr. La Quaglia and Cannon with the Divine Mercy of Christ, to give Cannon a chance to grow up and be a little boy and young man. Thank you.

Bit-By-Bit, Step-By-Step
Written Aug 3, 2013 8:32am

Good morning, and it is a good morning. Cannon is stable and resting.

We are in the PICU. Truly, right now, despite all the tubes, despite the major puffiness all over his body, I look at Cannon and I could not ever be more proud! He is my hero! An angel sent from God to Michael and me.

We are so thankful for all the prayers. Oh, how they work - Cannon is Exhibit A. I pray God's will is for Cannon to live, for Cannon to be a strong man and for us as a family to help fight childhood cancer with Cannon by our side.

Dr. L came in the parent room at around 9:15pm last night, after thirteen hours of surgery. As I stared at the doorknob, waiting for what seemed to be the longest day of my life, my stomach was in my mouth. The door slammed open and he said, "He is okay!", and he had a huge smile!!! Ahhhhhhhhh - can you hear my heart sing again? Instantly, the elephant that had been standing on my chest all day stopped!

He told me to sit down... I did as I was told! He stood there and it was a very different Dr. L. He looked really happy and proud of himself, and he should be. He said the tumor was extensive and that's why it took so long. He said it was unusual for it to be all the way down the pelvis to his legs, but it was, and he got down there all the way to his legs and scooped it out. Dr. L had previously said Cannon would need two surgeries to remove the mass, but he THINKS he got it all out. I wish I could show you how much gratitude I have in my heart! More than one could measure.

So for now, Cannon will stay mostly sedated and he is on a ventilator to breathe for him. But he is safe, his primary tumor is hopefully all out, and he is resting... all positives.

Seeing Cannon for the first time was not as hard as I thought it would be, mostly because all I wanted was to see him alive. Some families don't have the surgeon walk in and say he is okay! So I appreciate this blessing. I appreciate the fight.

Night Two In PICU
Written Aug 4, 2013 12:08am

Although now I look at Cannon, he is not really Cannon. He is puffy all over, his eyes are closed and huge and he is being kept alive by machines, BUT I know this: this, too, shall pass! I know he is in the best possible place with an amazing team of nurses looking after him twenty-four hours a day; they do not leave our room! They are my security blanket! I also know Dr. L exceeded his own expectations and was very proud, and that makes me proud.

I believe Cannon hears me so I talk to him often. I'm on the nightshift and Michael on the dayshift. It works great – I love my teammate. It was really hard to leave today and go back to the Ronald McDonald House for a sleep. I was sure I could not do it and Michael politely, but persuasively, suggested I go back and rest since I would again stay overnight.

My Hardest Day So Far Since This Journey Began
Written Aug 6, 2013 9:13pm

" The hardest day so far..."

Hard to believe, right? It wasn't the day he was diagnosed, it wasn't letting him go to surgery, it wasn't seeing him after surgery... it was today. Today was the hardest day for me since Cannon was diagnosed. It was in a word, BRUTAL.

Cannon was taken off the ventilator, but it wasn't smooth sailing. I watched as my son gasped for air, looking like he couldn't breathe over and over again. As the doctors smacked his back and held oxygen to his face, his levels dropped and they argued (stress-induced, of course) on what was the best course of action. Cannon tried to call out but his throat pain from the ventilator wouldn't allow it! So, he gasped and tears flowed over and over down his face. I wiped them away and told him Mummy was here, and I had to turn my head away as the tears ran down my cheeks. I couldn't fix it and my son was in despair, pain and shock! It was the most horrific thing I have ever seen! It was a pain I won't ever forget! For hours, it was touch-and-go with the oxygen and his levels; he had labored breathing for hours. Michael and my mum weren't at the hospital yet and watching them walk in was one of my happiest moments. I needed them and I haven't felt that way until today. I haven't felt I couldn't cope until today, my hardest day by far. I hope there are no more days where I don't know if Cannon will be okay. One word, brutal.

I explain in such detail because I want people to know neuroblastoma is no joke. It's no joke kids endure this and it must change!!!! I was determined before today but NOW I couldn't be more riled up to make changes! What Cannon and other kids endure is WRONG!!! And worse, it's not necessary!

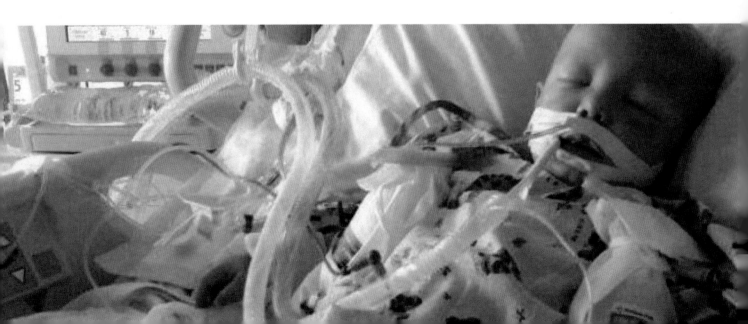

Another Day, Another Step - Blog By Dad, Michael Wiggins
Written Aug 7, 2013 7:24am

This morning Cannon is without energy and he is just worn out. I stand by his bed to make sure he doesn't pull out his oxygen line (I would rather stand here than put on the arm locks they want on him) and I look at him, and he looks back and all I see is, "Why?" I just tell him he's awesome and how proud I am of him, and then I just turn away, look out the window and ask the same question: Why?

I try to remind myself this is just one more day, and another step toward Cannon being cancer-free... a difficult mind trick from one day to the next. I can't say I have ever understood the concept of human suffering. I just don't get it. And, Cannon will turn two next week.

He Is Not Cannon
Written Aug 7, 2013 8:58pm

Cannon was moved this evening from ICU to POU, which is the Pediatric Observation Unit. There are three rooms and three nurses here.

Sadly, and with a heavy heart, I confess this post won't be the positive post I hoped it would be at this stage.

Cannon has not been himself. Expected? Yes!!! But, this is different. The way he has been is awful. His eyes roll back in his head all day, he can't focus on us or interact with us, he turns his head side-to-side, he can't focus on his iPad or his toys, he can't drink through a straw or his sippy cup properly, he can't hold his bottle, he can't hold up his head or body, and he is limp. He is NOT Cannon.

Michael, my mum and I have had a terrible time watching him this way. We have had doctors all over him and they believe he has delirium, which can happen in five percent of kids, post-op.

We haven't had that post-op smile or asking for a drink or wanting to watch his iPad! Nothing! He is not Cannon. The only way I can describe it is like he is mentally impaired. Like he isn't present. Like he doesn't know me or his dad or my mum! It's horrific, it's awful, it's a pain like no other. But, he is alive... so I will take it!

"I miss Cannon so very much!

Come back to me, Cannon.

Mumma misses your light in her life."

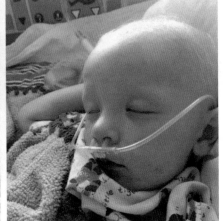

He Recognizes Us... Happy Second Birthday, Cannon!

Written Aug 10, 2013 10:20am

He recognizes us...

Tears, tears, tears of joy!!!!!!

Cannon smiled at Dad and me this morning! A gift from God!

I'm so happy I could burst!

Still a long road ahead but thankful for this moment! Living in this moment.

Happy birthday to the coolest two-year-old I know!

Love, Mum and Dad xoxox

A Letter From A Mother To Her Son

Written Aug 10, 2013 6:41pm

A birthday note...

Happy second birthday to the coolest two-year-old I know.

Despite all the heartache with Cannon's post-op complications, with breathing and hypo-active delirium, there is so much to be thankful for.

When Cannon turned one, I wrote him a letter and put it in a box for when he is eighteen. Here is my second birthday letter to my baby boy.

Dear Cannon,

It was two years ago today you came into this world. So much has happened. To start, you have two new brothers. In traditional Cannon fashion, you adore them. At first you threw the TV remote in their basket, but slowly you started to go over and rub their heads, and now you kiss their heads and put their bottles in their mouths - and sometimes you steal their bottles and drink them yourself. It's adorable! I have lots of pics to show you the proof!

Over these last two years since you came into my life, my life has changed forever. No one can love you like Dad and I do - we would die for you, sweet boy! But, you're special, you're something different. These past two years have been the happiest of my life! Nothing compares to the love for a child and you are my firstborn. I love you with every ounce of my being.

You're such a happy boy - I have many videos to prove it! Your most fav things right now are green smoothies, Mummy's breastmilk (sorry, LOL), hashbrowns (McDonald's - blame your father), Daddy's pasta, Mummy's chicken nuggets, iTunes videos (you're obsessed) and your most fav thing, OMG - swimming!!! Maybe now as you read this you swim in college, who knows?! Whatever you do, it will be great! I dread you leaving me and going to college (again, sorry, LOL). I'm sure as you read this you're 200 pounds and over six feet tall, like Dada!

All I know is today, and every day since you were born, I become more proud of you! You're a gift from God and no one is luckier than me to be your Mumma! I never take for granted what a gift that is to me! Never! You will do great things, Cannon - I believe that in my heart! You're a giver. You already share your food, kiss your brothers and cuddle your sissy. Your sweetness is something I admire so much. I see you helping so many people in your lifetime.

But with that comes a little price tag. You have been given a little challenge this year called cancer. I always knew you were special, Cannon, but in the past four months you have shown me God has BIG plans for you, and you're ready to do them. When you were 20 months old you were diagnosed with an ugly cancer called neuroblastoma. In simple terms, it has created soft and hard tissue tumors all over your body! Right now, you are in the FIGHT of your life and, just so you know, you don't come from a family where winning doesn't matter. It does! And this is the fight to win!!! You will win my baby! You will WIN!!!! You are the bravest little Braveheart I have ever seen!

Dad and I are right by your side and as we fight for you, we fight for others! Dad and I have learned so much about the terrible LACK of government funding and how many cancer charities only give one-cent on the dollar to children's cancer. Dad and I plan to change those numbers and we're working towards it for you and others!!! When you're better, you can help us and I know you are the kid who will want to help. You just are!

This last year you have walked, yelled a lot, swam, ran and done so much! You have been to Scotland - which you loved!!! Beach trips with your BFF Brendan, Disney trips... you have run Mum and Dad ragged and we have LOVED every single second!

I am not sure what the next year holds and don't need to know. But I know today Dad and I will give you the best birthday we possibly can! You're our angel sent from God and we love you more than life itself!

Happy birthday, my baby boy!
Mumma loves you!
Love, Big Mumma Wiggins

The Giggle Is Back, Baby! Nine Days Post-Op, Fifth Round Of Chemo
Written Aug 11, 2013 6:32pm

Today, I find myself mystified by Cannon, but really I shouldn't be. The kid is incredible. I got Cannon out of bed, a very delicate procedure because of his incision, and we went to the playroom. Being the pushy mum (at least I admit it), I took him out of the wagon and put him on the floor (that didn't make him too happy). I pretended I didn't understand why he was upset and proceeded to get out the remote control cars I bought him, and I drove them crazily around the family room and ran them into walls and sofas and there, in that moment, it happened. He giggled... hard. He looked at me like, "Why did you stop, Mum?" I was choked up. I kissed his head and I relished that moment. Only a day before he did not recognize me. The pain of having Cannon not know me was agony. I thought about families with kids who have lost their memories from such things as accidents or disease and I prayed for them. Cannon was like that, but it lasted eight days. For some families, it lasts forever. I am so choked up with gratitude today. I know things could have been so much worse. So, yes, does it stink Cannon starts his fifth round of chemo tomorrow? It sure does, but at least he can get mad about it and at least he will show emotion and feel comfort in having his Mum and Dada with him. My baby came back to me... a gift from God. How do I say thanks for my son coming back to me? The only way I know how... keep fighting hard and helping others. While Cannon and I were playing, he tried to stand up. He couldn't, he didn't have the strength, so I helped him up. I held his hands above his head and he led me to the door then pushed my hand to the door to open it. I did! Cannon then led me to walk around the floor. That's right, walk (albeit I held both his hands)! He wanted to walk (first time in ten days) and it wasn't pushy Mum, it was ALL him! As I said, he amazes me, but I shouldn't be amazed. He is quite simply the coolest two year old I know.

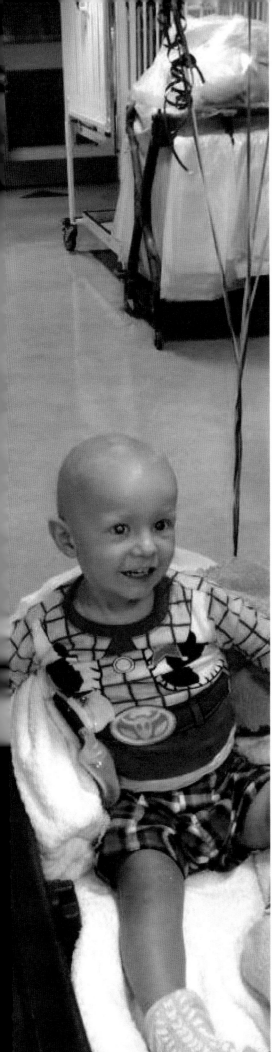

Almost Home: Goodbye New York, Hello Orlando
Written Aug 15, 2013 4:51pm

Cannon will have his last day of chemo here today and we are hoping and praying we can fly home Saturday afternoon. It's given Michael and me a spring in our steps to think about going home to our kids. We miss them. I recall a friend saying, "Bring him back". Well, we are!! Does Cannon still have cancer? Yes, he does. But are we picking it off bit-by-bit? You bet we are! Cannon is killing it!!! What's new, huh?? Quite the showoff, my son. I have no idea where he gets it. :) I can't explain in words the gratitude I have that we are bringing Cannon home. I know this is not always how it goes for families and it could be very different. It's why I say "Thankful for the fight." I am! So thankful! For the mother who received a call her child drowned, for the father who received a call his daughter died in a car accident, I promise to fight hard and do it with gratitude, for I know if you could be in my shoes you would! I think of you parents daily!!! Daily!

Keep praying for Cannon. Chemo is rough, as always, but he will get through this. This, too, shall pass! Michael and I are really pushing him hard to walk. He, in typical toddler style, falls to the ground and stomps his feet. Ok, he may have inherited that one from me. What? At least I admit it. But Michael and I keep pushing and pushing. Neither of us are quitters, I think it's our sport backgrounds.

Praying we sleep in our own beds Saturday night!

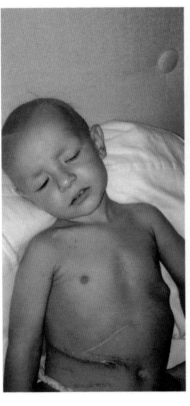

Homeward Bound... Two Weeks Post-Surgery
Written Aug 17, 2013 3:30pm

Deep breaths, we made it. We are on the plane.

Finally, we are on the plane. I must confess, last night was a rough night and this morning has been worse (vomit in the car to airport, vomit at the airport, vomit at security) and this Scottish lass without sleep and food, well, let's just say the lady behind me who is bitching about not being able to sit beside her husband on a three hour flight better pipe down... LOL.

I also confess I'm emotionally spent and I know Michael is, too. I've never experienced three weeks like that in my life. I can't imagine what poor baby Cannon feels like. I just know that no fresh air for two weeks and no train set are pretty darn miserable for him.

It's hard to believe that two weeks ago Cannon underwent thirteen hours of surgery to remove the primary tumor in his stomach. It's hard to believe he was on life support for five days. It's hard to believe it felt like we were losing him when he was being taken off the ventilator. And, it's hard to believe he didn't recognize us for eight days. But then, I know how tired and worn out I feel and it doesn't feel so hard to believe.

As tired and as worn out we all feel as a family, there is so much love and peace in our hearts because we are on a plane with OUR baby. I remember writing on the way up here and thinking all I wanted was to bring my baby home alive and that wish came true! So, we will take the vomit, the ventilators, the delirium, the meds, the fact he can't walk, the blood transfusion he had at 4am last night. We will take every single bit of it because our baby is alive!

A Mother's Worst Nightmare
Written Aug 22, 2013 2:17pm

Many people say to me I'm living every mother's/parent's worst nightmare... I'm not! Actually, my worst nightmare would have been a call that my son died in a car crash, or my son had six months to live, or he drowned in a pool! I'm actually one of the lucky mums. Why? Because I get to fight!!! Not a day goes past I don't FEEL or believe it! Is it hard? You bet it is! It's brutal! It's painful! I walk around all day with what feels like an elephant on my chest. It hurts to take a deep breath most days.

Michael and I have seen but a few smiles since surgery, and Cannon's smiles are our medicine. We're both sick without them! We miss them! We miss little Cannonball!

I won't deny this week has been challenging for me. Watching Cannon so unwell is painful! You know the book series, "...For the Soul"? Cannon's smile and personality fill my soul! And I feel empty! Looking after Cannon with him not able to walk, and with him having vomit and diarrhea while taking care of the twins is a challenge. I am exhausted as you can imagine, but I know if I could just see some smiles and the twinkle in Cannon's eyes I could feed my soul and my spirit! I could use a lift... we all could!

Broken Spirit
Written Aug 25, 2013 10:08am

Difficult to type, but SADLY it's the truth.

Cannon has a broken spirit.

He is listless. He doesn't smile, he doesn't giggle, he doesn't want to move... ever. If he eats, he vomits it up. Fourteen days of vomit on top of a thirteen hour surgery has just broken him! He acts like he doesn't care if he is here or not, and that he has given up the fight. It's heartbreaking!!

I even took him in the pool yesterday and he screamed. He was so mad at me. He hated it. Anyone who knows my baby knows swimming is where it's at for him. I pretended I didn't understand. He hated it and that made him mad. On a positive note, I did that as he kicked his legs and that will help him get strong. I plan on doing it again, despite the fact it makes him mad. In the words of my father... cruel to be kind.

We got out of the hospital Friday around 5:30pm and we were back at the hospital again by 7pm. He is out now and we will have to take him back in. He just isn't doing well at all. Cannon doesn't have a life right now. He isn't living, he is existing. We miss his smile and giggle, but we are thankful for the fight.

Pray Hard
Written Aug 28, 2013 10:28am

Cannon is making no improvements. In fact, the doctors think he is worse since being admitted. They are worried. Michael has a gut feeling something is wrong.

We are doing a CT of his brain to see if anything is wrong. I am so scared I could vomit! I am struggling to keep it together in this moment but I know prayers will help Cannon, Michael and me!

I beg of you,
Pray,
Pray hard!

We need clear scans.

Cannon needs them.

I don't want to lose my baby.

My heart is breaking right now.

I know I need to live in the moment and wait until results come in... but Cannon is very sick and it's painful beyond belief to watch.

I want to believe it's just the effects of post-surgery/chemo, but our hearts are in fear.

I am staying strong for Cannon, but my heart is aching.

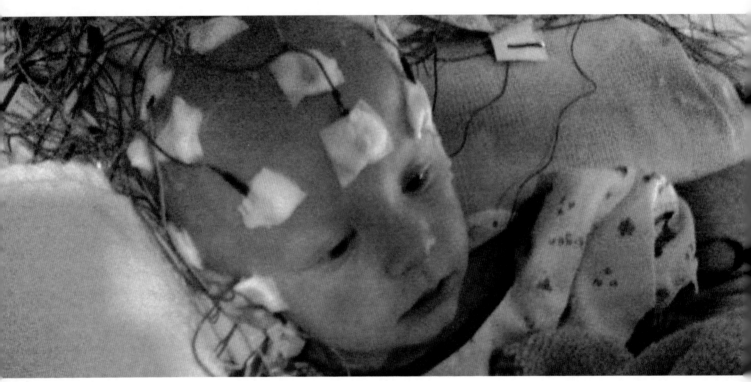

Your Prayers Worked... AGAIN
Written Aug 28, 2013 6:24pm

I believe... I have always believed but never has my faith been stronger or have I felt more connected in prayer than these days.

You all prayed...

Clear scans...

No neuroblastoma or other issues in the brain. I just want to live in this moment of pure gratitude.

September 1st 2013

136 DAYS

SINCE DIAGNOSIS

Two-thirds of childhood cancer patients
will have long lasting chronic conditions
from treatment.

*Source: Alex's Lemonade Stand

September Is Here: Childhood cancer Awareness Month - Blog By Dad, Michael Wiggins
Written Sep 12, 2013 10:05pm

September is recognized in the U.S. as Childhood cancer Awareness Month. Those who have read our posts and followed Cannon since his diagnosis with stage four neuroblastoma in April, know Melissa and I have committed ourselves now, and in our forever futures, to help rid the world of cancer striking kids.

We know at this time, with Cannon fully engaged in treatment and beating this horrible disease, our best efforts will be for raising awareness to start, and then move to full action once Cannon is cancer-free. I have told others personally, and I will state it here again, and I hope anyone who reads this holds me to it and reminds me if I ever appear to slip up or slow down: I will spend the rest of my life fighting for these kids with cancer. The near barbaric treatment and daily pain and misery innocent children suffer resulting from cancer is as unjust a cause as any I have known, seen or experienced. I challenge anyone to show me more suffering that is unjust and unnecessary and avoidable in fully-developed countries with so-called modern medicine and medical research.

Families, charities and research groups across the United States observe September as Childhood cancer Awareness Month. Let's do the job here in the U.S. and spread the word to the U.K., and other parts of the world. A diagnosis of cancer turns the lives of the entire family upside down.

The objective of Childhood cancer Awareness Month is to put a spotlight on the types of cancers which largely affect children, survivorship issues, and - importantly - to help raise funds for research and family support.

In 2012, September was proclaimed Childhood cancer Awareness Month across the U.S., by stating, in part: "The causes of pediatric cancer are still largely unknown, and though new discoveries are resulting in new treatments, this heartbreaking disease continues to scar families and communities in ways that may never fully heal. This month, we remember the young lives taken too soon, stand with the families facing childhood cancer today, and rededicate ourselves to combating this terrible illness."

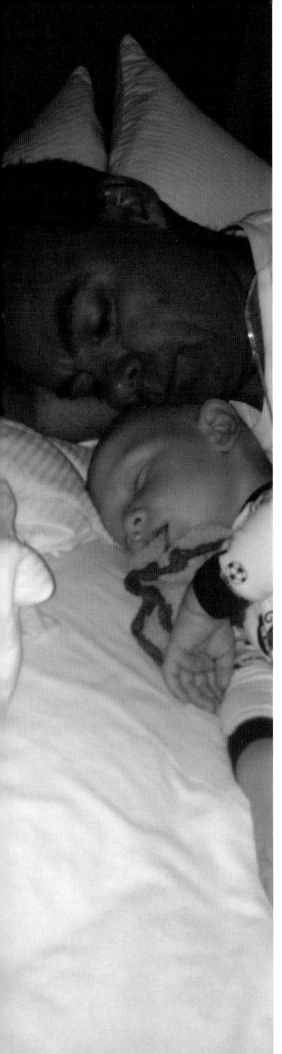

Don't Ask Why
Written Aug 15, 2013 4:51pm

I don't want to be the person that asks why. I don't want to be the person who says it's unfair. I do, however, want to be the person who says I did everything in my power to save my son's life... EVERYTHING... and it worked and he is saved!!!!

This evening I got to spend time with a woman I hope to be like someday - Miss Mary Parker. To say she is amazing doesn't quite do her justice. She is a true inspiration to me for so many reasons. Mary made a great analogy tonight. She said, "It's like your son has been captured and you're with him, but they say you need to sit and watch him be tortured and they may or may not let you go free. If they do, they may or may not come looking for him again." I thought that was an amazing analogy for what this beast, cancer, has done to our son. Day after day, we watch our son in pain. Like today, seeing the horror on his face as we entered the clinic for labs, or seeing him cry his eyes out to leave as he is sick of the hospital, or seeing the pain in his eyes as I clean his bottom because it hurts so bad, or seeing how mad he is because I took him out to walk around the lake. Cannon's days, and his emotions, are like a roller coaster. Today, he had a bad case of vomit all over me, my sister Nicole and everything else in sight. Cannon cried mostly from embarrassment, not from the pain. He hates to see us clean it and his eyes look like he is ashamed. It's gut-wrenching, as he only turned two a month ago. Later, he came up to me and looked the same way, sad and very concerned. I asked him what was wrong, but he can't talk, so he didn't say anything. Then I saw it... there was diarrhea running down his leg and all over the sofa and on his hands. Trust me, I would clean up anything for this angel of mine, but it makes him sad and upset and he looks ashamed, and that hurts me more than anything. I don't know how to help him from feeling ashamed, aside from telling him constantly, "It's okay" and "No worries", and how much I love him.

Michael and I haven't stopped since that day on April 19, 2013. We will never, ever stop fighting for our baby! Never. The scary part of neuroblastoma is there is no set path for treatment.

Some schools of thought are to do stem cell transplant and some are not. Some use certain drugs and others don't. I said it at the beginning of this blog - I never, ever want to have regrets. I never want to think I didn't do enough! So, at every step of Cannon's treatment, Michael and I huddle up like it's half-time at the national championship game, and we review the play so far and we research what's next. That's where we are now - stem cell and drugs. To say this is a huge, huge decision is an understatement. Kids die during transplant. Sometimes their bodies can't take it, sometimes their veins give up and they die. As I type that word, I feel like an elephant is sitting on my chest. Please pray Michael and I make the right decision for our baby boy and we continue to work as team and come to the same decision on how to move forward.

Tests And Scans - Blog By Dad, Michael Wiggins
Written Sep 25, 2013 8:06am

This morning, Cannon is off to APHC to begin a series of post-round six chemotherapy tests and scans. He will have an echocardiogram this morning to continually monitor his heart and to ensure heart health as we head towards autologous stem cell transplant (ASCT), beginning on October 14. Tomorrow, he will have a CT scan of his abdomen and pelvis to see what solid tumor, if any, is remaining after the surgery by Dr. La Quaglia in August, and he will have another MIBG scan, which detects neuroblastoma cells that still may be in his body. Friday, he will have another bone marrow biopsy to see whether any new cancer cells are in his bone marrow or if any have returned there.

Not NED... No RELAPSE
Written Sep 26, 2013 9:15pm

Apologies for the delay... it always takes me a minute to process things when it comes to Cannon.

First of all, I am very thankful my son is alive after six rounds of chemo, three surgeries, life support, delirium and everything else he has endured!!!! This is not always the case with stage four neuroblastoma, so this is a gift for me and my family!

Second, Cannon is not NED. Is this what we want? No. Is it okay? Yes! It's okay not to be NED right now because although seventy-five percent or more of kids are NED at this point, seventy-five percent of kids aren't half-Scottish, half-American, and seventy-five percent of kids aren't Cannon Wiggins. That's right... have you met this kid? He is special. He is a very, very special kid! And I don't say this because he is mine, although it sounds that way. It's very difficult to explain in words how much of a beautiful soul this child is, how gentle, how inspiring, how wonderfully caring he is unless you have been around him long enough to see it in his eyes. You can't really relate - just take my word for it! He is an angel. I am happy to share with all of you this angel of mine and, someday, I hope you all get to see his true beauty in person. So, yes, he is not NED like a lot of kids, but that's okay because he is Cannon Wiggins and God knew he could handle this little extra challenge! And he can! I believe in you, Cannon Wiggins.

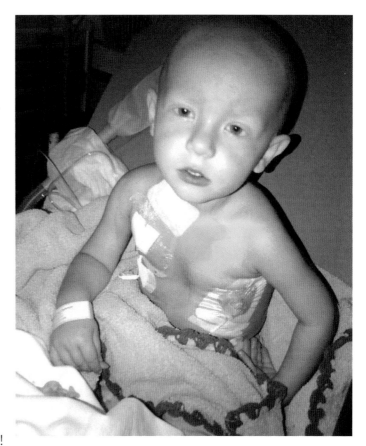

Third, although we are not NED, we are not in relapse (two to five percent chance of survival), something to be very, very, very thankful for! Cannon still has active neuroblastoma cells in his leg – "stubborn leg", we call it now!

A New Hero - Blog By Dad, Michael Wiggins
Written Sep 30, 2013 7:10am

Today is the last day of September, and the last day of Childhood cancer Awareness Month.

Over the past month, Melissa and I have detailed Cannon's continuing journey, our return and continuing rehabilitation from his surgery in New York, his fifth and sixth rounds of chemotherapy, stays at APHC including his nearly one week stay for a post-chemo fever, his twice-a-week trips to the outpatient clinic, his blood and platelet transfusions, and his good days and not so good days. He's had days of play and smiles, but he's had more days of nausea, severe vomiting, diarrhea, pain from his incision, pain from his medications, being continuously awakened during the night while in the hospital by nurses doing their jobs or by me at home, having to sit up while sleeping to have horrible medicines injected in his mouth at intervals during the night, and having needle biopsies and radiation scans that required sedation. And, not to forget, all the daily needle injections we had to give him at home, sometimes twice. And that was just September.

When I was a kid, my hero was a baseball player named Mike Schmidt. Mike Schmidt played third base for the Philadelphia Phillies in the 1970's and 80's, and was a Major League All-Star in twelve different years, hit 548 career home runs and is now in the Baseball Hall of Fame. Even as an adult, I always said my hero was Mike Schmidt.

I have a new hero in my life. In fact, many new ones. It is Cannon, and all the kids who suffer from cancer. I have witnessed so many of them screaming in pain, crying in the middle of the night or early in the morning, exhausted because of continual sticking, prodding and examining, vomiting in their sleep and the fear in their eyes that no child should experience. I have said before, I truly don't understand human suffering. I just don't get it. Even more so, when it is children who suffer. The admiration I have for these kids is beyond my ability to describe. It has brought tears to my eyes.

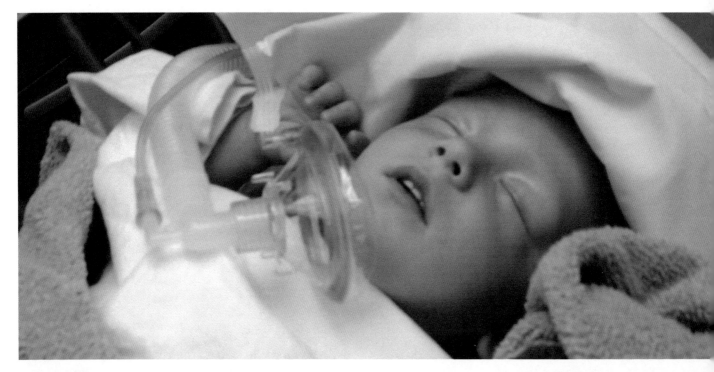

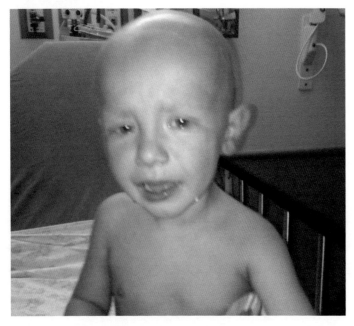

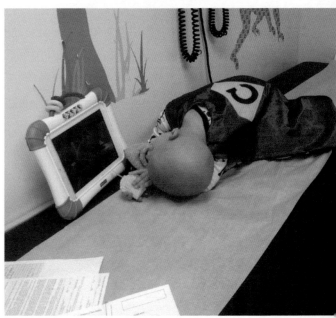

October 3rd 2013

168 DAYS

SINCE DIAGNOSIS

A child's developing and growing body and organs respond differently to "hand-me-down" chemotherapy drugs used on adults. Drugs designed, tested and approved for adults, especially those so drastic in intent, should not have to be used on children, yet they are in kids with cancer... almost predominantly.

*Source: People Against Childhood Cancer

First Breath In Five Months: A Short Family Vacation Before Stem Cell Transplant

Written Oct 3, 2013 10:10pm

Can you hear that? It's me breathing easy ...

We are at a house in Anna Maria Island – it's pure heaven. It has a beautiful dock and a pool and hot tub. The beach is ten minutes away. As I type, everyone is asleep. Yes, everyone - babies, Cannon, my sister Nicole - and all is quiet in this beautiful home. I like it here. There is no medicine in the fridge like our home, there aren't posters from the hospital, there aren't wipes which remind me of the hospital, there are no needles for injections and there is no TPN monitor. There are no reminders my baby has cancer. I feel like, for the first time in five months, I can breathe, and trust me, I am soaking in every single breath of the sea air. I am storing every breath for transplant and for building Cannon and myself up for the next battle, to which there are many in this WAR against cancer.

I feel this week has allowed me to take a minute, breathe and see things clearly. Truly, I feel like I am just getting over the trauma of what I saw my baby endure in New York. I wish I could forget it some days but I can't. There isn't a day I do.

Breathing easy has made me see clearly. This week, I asked myself the question, "If Shands and the Children's Hospital of Philadelphia (CHOP) were right in front of me in Orlando, where would I choose to do stem cell transplant?" I asked Michael the same question. I think Michael and I have been so worn out by this process, and especially New York, we didn't really look at CHOP like we SHOULD have. As a result, I am shortening our vacation and going to Philly on Monday with Michael to meet with Dr. Stephan Grupp, the Medical Director of the Stem Cell Laboratory at CHOP. We will fly up Monday (the kids will stay in Orlando) and fly back Tuesday evening. My gut is telling me CHOP is the place to go, and I cannot go forward with Shands without following my gut and looking into it. Michael, as always, is supportive of me and I don't know what I would do without that man – I'd be lost.

One Step Closer
Written Oct 6, 2013 9:53pm

We honestly had the most incredible week! I was burned out upon our arrival at the beach. Upon my return I am energized, pumped up, eager and ready to get my incredible Cannonball to NED!!!!

As I sit here, I am preparing my questions for the CHOP transplant team - I have many! Two lawyers... poor doctors.

Praying we have the answers we need to commence transplant on October 14.

Cannon is fattening up. His spirit is strong, he is ready!!! We are ready!!!

Our Day At CHOP... Our Decision
Written Oct 7, 2013 8:25pm

We just met with the head transplant guy here, Dr. Grupp. Wow!!!! The intelligence literally seeps out of this guy! I truly enjoyed (yes, enjoyed) the one hour we spent with him! I had so many questions and he did for us, too! I loved that! I learned so much about nb and stem cell transplant and why it's right for our baby. I soaked up every bit of info!

Next, the social worker and the nurses gave us a tour of where Cannon would stay.

Michael and I went back to the room and took a break for an hour before heading to dinner. At dinner, Michael and I were at a complete consensus. We are going to CHOP!!!!

The plan of action is rolling and it's all happening so fast. Cannon and I will travel back to Philly on Thursday. Friday, Cannon will go through a period of tests to ensure everything is working good to go ahead with transplant. Monday he will have a line placed and Tuesday he will begin. Michael will join us Saturday and my sister, mum and twins next week.

So, you can imagine what needs to be organized tomorrow and Wednesday. My list is endless. We could be away from home for two months depending on what we decide about radiation. Radiation happens right after stem cell transplant!

Stem Cell Transplant Begins - Children's Hospital Of Philadelphia -- Pennsylvania
Written Oct 15, 2013 10:06am

This morning was hard. Cannon was so cuddly in his onesie (I know he is two, but they are just too cute) and he was cuddling into Dad and me in bed. I kept him in his PJ's so I didn't need to wake him up so much. As I got ready, Dad and Cannon cuddled up. Tears rolled down Dad's face as Cannon slept. My heart broke over and over again. Our baby is so happy right now and it is beyond painful to take him to the hospital today.

As I walked to the hospital (Michael stayed at the hotel to deal with all the real life things: accommodations, supplies for transplant, washing clothes, etc.), I was choked up. I was thinking that the next time I stay at the hotel Cannon won't be there, and how very sad that was. Cannon is my buddy, my partner in crime and he makes anything fun!

I know I need to think this is what's best, this is next in the protocol for stage four neuroblastoma and this is what many parents choose for their kids. Without transplant, Cannon won't make it. I know all that. But today, in this moment, I'm just sad. I'm sad my happy boy yesterday is now crying in my arms because he wants to eat and drink and he can't because he has to be put under for a line to be placed in his chest. He keeps signing to me saying, "Food, food, food!" Painful!! So unfair and so hard to watch! So today, I am just sad and tomorrow I will be back in fighting mode, I'm sure! But today, my heart hurts for my baby boy, for my husband and for all who suffer from cancer.

Hotel... Alone, Hearing Loss
Written Oct 15, 2013 9:34pm

I'm back at the hotel ALONE while Cannon and Dada are at the hospital. The room is just lifeless. No Cannon running around smiling and laughing and playing! I am not sure whether it's easier being at the hospital or away! Either way you worry... CONSTANTLY!!

I am doing laundry now as everything can only be worn once, then it needs to be washed to keep Cannon safe from germs.

Today was rough...

Dr. Grupp called me and said he needed to talk to me. He said Cannon's last audiogram showed, in his words, significant hearing loss. He told me he was sorry and he wished he had different news. I knew Cannon had lost hearing, I told Michael as much. After this round of chemo, starting tomorrow at 8am, Cannon will require hearing aids. This round of chemo will have a significant effect on Cannon's hearing!! He continued to explain that because Cannon is so young he will have speech problems, too! In that moment, when he told me he was sorry, I said, "I want my son alive, that's job number one. All the rest is secondary."

It is secondary...

With that said, I kind of feel like I'm mourning today. I'm mourning the life I dreamt of for my son. I don't want Cannon to go through this two year protocol only to deal with bullies who will make fun of him for his speech or his height or his hearing aids. I don't want him to be sad when he finds out he can't make his own little Cannonballs! I have never written these words before, but today I will!!

CANCER SUCKS!!!!!! It really sucks for these kids!!! They fight for their lives only to deal with issues their whole lives! It makes me hurt so hard in my heart for him! My heart literally feels like it's breaking so hard!

Please Pray - Six Months Since Diagnosis
Written Oct 18, 2013 7:43pm v

Tomorrow morning they will, God willing, hang the last bag of chemo for Cannon ever in his life!!!!!!!

I have tears rolling down my face just typing those words. To think of this stem cell transplant saving Cannon's life and getting him to NED - that's the goal!!!!! Please God, make it so.

So once again, I ask for your prayers. Once again, I ask you pray hard for my baby boy. Once again, I ask you pray this treatment saves his life!!!!

Tomorrow is the six month mark since the day we were told, "Your son has stage four neuroblastoma cancer."

In six months, Cannon has had three surgeries, one which was thirteen hours long, life support for five days, delirium, six rounds of chemo, more chemo and now transplant! He has so much still to do including radiation, antibodies, immunotherapy... all this by the age of just turning two.

This is the most painful roller coaster ride of our life! But we're ready cancer, bring it on! Give us your best because Cannonball is leading the army and his prayer warriors are right behind him!!!!

Monday Morning Blues: One Week Into Stem Cell Transplant - Blog By Dad, Michael Wiggins

Written Oct 21, 2013 7:31am

This morning Cannon reaches almost one week into the stem cell transplant process. The chemo is over, but the misery - burning insides, mouth sores, feeling very poorly and weak - has just begun. We've been told by the doctors the next two weeks will be difficult for Cannon. I ask myself when I hear that, "Compared to what? Like the hell and torture he's already had or even more?"

What A Difference A Week Makes, Blood Donations

Written Oct 24, 2013 7:45am

Cannon had a rough night with vomiting a lot of blood. He may need blood and/or platelets today. Did you know when you donated blood you would be saving my son? You are!!!! Our kids on this transplant floor couldn't survive without you. My deepest, deepest gratitude.

Cannon had so much diarrhea yesterday that I lost count of the loads of wash and of the times I changed his bed.

" I told him 'This is what you're fighting for.'"

I hardly slept last night because even when Cannon was sleeping I couldn't, as I'm so scared he might choke on his vomit.

Cannon is fighting so hard. Last night, despite his non-responsive attitude, I played videos of him and Dad playing ball and us at the park to show him what he is fighting for! I also have fun pictures all over the room walls to remind him!!!! I told him "This is what you're fighting for."

"Why, Mum?"

Written Oct 26, 2013 5:40pm

Today I watched tears roll down my son's face and watched the torture on his face from the pain the chemo has created in his body! Cannon is very agitated and doesn't know what he wants and makes noises. He is in constant pain despite his morphine drip! We are in the thick of things and it's painful to watch your child look at you like, "Why, Mum? Fix it, Mum." Sheer despair in his eyes! But I fight! And I fight hard! I will never, ever, ever give up for Cannon and all the others!

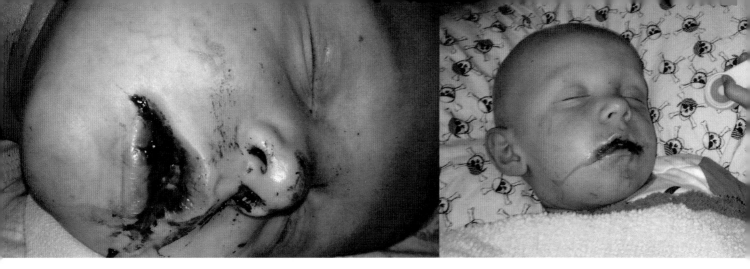

Video Controversy... Creating Awareness
Written Oct 28, 2013 5:31pm

My short video (posted Oct. 26) of Cannon in his current state, has sparked much controversy about the REALITY of childhood cancer. I have said it before, and I will say it over and over, as painful as it is to take the video and post it, my feelings are secondary and raising awareness and increasing blood donations are primary! If this short video sparked some controversy and made people say, "Enough! What can I do?", then I'm fulfilling my role as a mother whose child is fighting every second of his life to beat cancer, and he is only two. He is one of thousands! It's not right and it must change! It can! I pray it will! I will fight until the day I die that it does!!!!

Did you watch the video?
Do you want to do something?
I have some ideas:
· Share Cannon's page
· Share the video
· Wear a Cannonball Kids' cancer T-shirt to spark conversation
· Contact your local elementary school and ask to do a short presentation. What could be more effective than kids spreading the message about kids' cancer - like Princeton Elementary is doing so humbly?!
· Donate blood - Cannon is receiving blood daily to stay alive right now!
· Pray - pray hard!!!!!! The power of prayer is unbelievable to me!
· Donate to a cancer organization that supports kids' cancer. Some I like are St. Baldrick's and Alex's Lemonade Stand!

Cannon is much the same but is now on a breathing cannula which supplies him with oxygen. His oxygen levels kept dropping last night and it was really worrying. I was actually resting at the hotel and went back to the hospital because it freaks me out whenever his oxygen gets low as it can lead to brain damage. Cannon's tiny body is just fighting so hard. I'm thankful he can have some oxygen that will help him breathe, bring down his heart rate and make him work just a little less hard! Praying every minute for NED!!

Cannon, Transplant, And A Note To The Haters

Written Oct 29, 2013 5:59pm

Cannon and I have spent the day together. I've had him out of bed quite a bit - much to his displeasure! I think you all know this, but I am definitely the bad cop parent. ;) But, Cannon is so lucky to have his daddy who comforts him in a way I have never seen a father and son interact. I loved my husband before, but my level of love and appreciation has reached a new level! Cannon is a lucky boy to have his daddy!

I gave Cannon his first bath in two weeks today. Splashing in the water brought back happy memories and as I washed his back, I fought so hard and managed to keep my tears from falling! Cannon cannot see me cry! I am his rock! I will always be his rock! My family's rock! That's my job! I take my work very seriously! But Cannon's skin is almost see-through; it's peeling off, cut up, burned, and so, so tender! His skin around his diaper area is peeling off and literally red raw! I was being so gentle (not a natural instinct to me due to my father ;)) but he cried the entire time and was scared. The fear in his face was heartbreaking to watch! He must be bathed as he now has more ability to sit up! Bacteria can get on his skin and an infection to Cannon is fatal right now! That's not an exaggeration. Thus, he must be washed daily, despite the pain it causes him.

Today I met with the nurse practitioner who educates parents on post-transplant care. To summarize, Cannon basically will be in isolation in our home for six months (when not in treatment), with no visitors. No public places! Brutal for a two-year-old for so many reasons, including his development.

We have been told Cannon will have hearing aids after transplant. Today I was looking at him thinking, "Are these the last days he will hear my voice without help?" My insides feel thoroughly beaten up the past two weeks. Can you imagine what Cannon feels like?

A sidenote to all the haters, LOL. Some nasty comments I have received, like I am a bad mother, are very sad, but I will say this: the video I showed was mild! That was a good moment for Cannon! Perhaps I could post him screaming as I bathe him or me pinning him down while a nurse suctions his mouth as he screams with pain and blood pours from his mouth? This is Cannon's reality! I showed a video of an easy part of his day to show people how he was doing and to create awareness and encourage blood donations. I believe I'm doing what God has intended! I am a firm, firm believer that from every bad must come good. I hope I am doing some good because it is always my intention! Always!

Please keep praying for baby Cannonball!

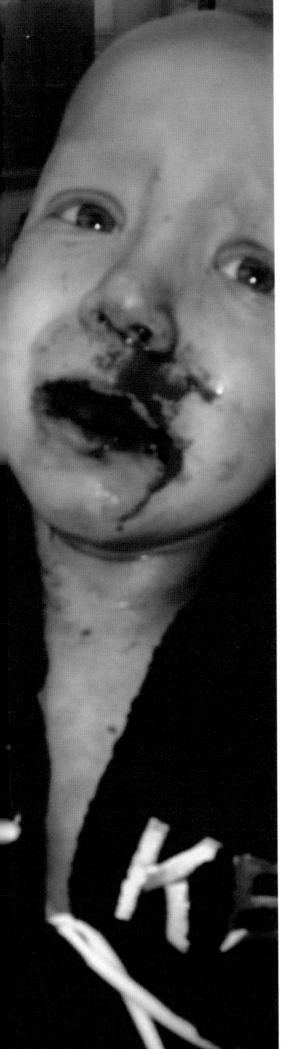

This Is What cancer In Kids Looks Like
Written Oct 30, 2013 9:04pm

Cannon is in the thick of it... day plus seven post-transplant. They say days six through eleven are tough and the closer the child gets to day fourteen the better they feel. Roll on day fourteen!

Today we couldn't get Cannon to stop bleeding from his nose. He had platelets and blood to help with that. The nosebleeds are caused by really low platelets. Basically, during transplant the kids are taken as close to death as possible – strangely, to save their lives. I'm praying hard for NED after stem cell. Then... can I say it? All this pain he endures would be worth it!!

Neuroblastoma is said to be the hardest childhood cancer to beat. More kids five years old and younger die from neuroblastoma than any other cancer or disease in the world. That's both terrifying and horrific, all at the same time. I tell you this because, as absolutely heart wrenching as it is for me to post the pictures of Cannon feeling so unwell, I do it because I NEED your help. I need you to know what these kids go through and I hope it puts a fire in your belly to move to action. Any action... all action counts!

I need all of you to help our family. You can create awareness, hold a blood drive, give blood. You are all amazing me daily with the good in people and the love people can have for someone that many of you have never met. I never knew that was possible!

These kids need you. Trust my word on that! Take action so more kids don't have to go through what Cannon and others do daily. These pictures are just one day in the life of a kid with cancer. Today! We only have today!

November 1st 2013

197 DAYS

SINCE DIAGNOSIS

Childhood cancer is not just one disease.
It is made up of a dozen types
and countless subtypes.

*Source: Alex's Lemonade Stand

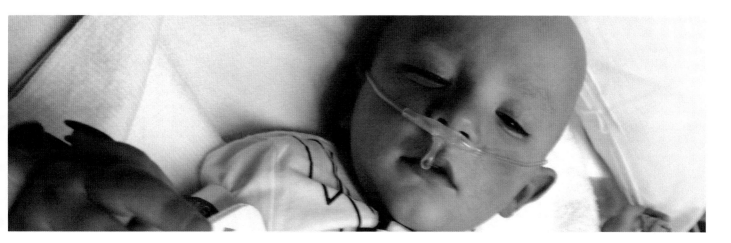

A Letter To Cannon
Written Nov 1, 2013 10:28pm

I write tonight with lumps in my throat, pain in my heart and tears in my eyes.

Sometimes the pain of watching my child be so sick is so unbearable I feel my heart is literally going to shatter into a million pieces.

Dear Cannon, my baby boy,

I miss you, baby.
I miss your smile.
I miss your giggle.
I miss you biting my toes.
I miss playing hide-and-seek.
I miss seeing you run and bang your hands on the mirror and giggle at your reflection.
I miss seeing you and Dada play.
I miss seeing you and Auntie Nicole in the pool.
I miss having a healthy son.
I miss teaching you flashcards.
I miss seeing your face when you see trains.
And, I miss seeing you jump in the splash pads.

I know you're busy, Cannon.
You're fighting so hard inside, so we can't do all these things.
But, boy-oh-boy, I miss you!

You're fighting so hard, so we can do all those things forever and ever.
And, nobody fights like you do, kiddo.
I never saw anyone fight so hard to live.

Mumma misses our time together so much. I will try to be brave just like you and work hard to help other kids like you, too!

You've got this, Cannon.
I can't wait to play soon.
I love you to infinity and beyond!

Your Mumma-Bear Wiggins

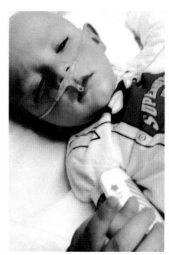

Emotionally Spent: Goodbye Mum And Twins

Written Nov 9, 2013 10:08pm

It's been a really emotional week for so many reasons. Sometimes there is only so much you can take when you watch your son suffer incomprehensibly day-in and day-out. Cannon is improving, but not at the pace this impatient Scottish lassy would like.

This week has been especially challenging. A combination of things, including saying goodbye to my mum who is headed back to Scotland, and to my twin baby boys who went back to Orlando. Both really tugged at my heartstrings. My mum has been a saint with the twins. Thank goodness she was here as I couldn't handle being away from them that long. My heart aches for them.

Cannon is staying pretty steady. He is having daily transfusions and we are still trying to have him eat and drink (though failing miserably). Please pray Cannon can eat or drink this week. If only I could explain to him he can't get out of isolation until he does.

Progressing - Blog By Dad, Michael Wiggins

Written Nov 10, 2013 10:02am

Cannon is progressing. That's the best word I can offer for now. I truly won't say he is "better" (although in the true sense of the definition, that is probably correct), because he is not healed from the burns all inside his mouth, lips, throat, stomach, his entire bottom and private areas. It is not as bad as last week, but far from normal or what anyone could live with normally. The mucositis still persists. Those who have experienced mucositis or have seen it can relate to this. It is horrible. So much mucous builds up in the mouth and throat; it nearly prevents breathing and won't stop. It is vomited in large balls a couple of times a day, or awakens Cannon and scares him because he was asleep. It is so thick I can grab some with a tissue at the edge of Cannon's mouth and roll the tissue and pull it out continuously, like yarn on a spool. Cannon cries when we do this and other suctioning to get it out, but it helps him clear his mouth and throat and relieves some of his misery. We usually hit the pain pump before or after we do this, and I say "progressing", because now we only hit the pain pump for Cannon about five times a day, compared with last week, and the week before, at multiples of that number. So, to sum up and reply to those who graciously ask how Cannon is doing, I say his counts are higher and he is progressing, and is one day closer to being cancer-free. We look forward to Cannon coming back to us, and seeing our first smile and giggle in more than a month (I heard this morning that it might be today).

" We look forward to Cannon coming back to us, and seeing our first smile and giggle in more than a month."

Backwards Not Forwards

Written Nov 12, 2013 4:56pm

Michael and Cannon had a really rough night. My heart ached as Michael gave me the rundown on their painful night. Cannon had walked for me the day before, yet he couldn't even walk a few steps for Michael. He was bent over in pain and limping, he cried and ached all night and Michael grew really concerned. Michael pulled the team (doctor, charge nurse, etc.) in the room at 3am (I love that man so much). When it comes to our children, he doesn't give a crap if he upsets anyone or what people think of him. It's truly one of the things I love most about this man whom I call my husband (ok, before I make you all sick, I will stop).

They decided he needed a CT of his stomach area in case he had an infection. Michael had to leave for Orlando first thing, so I took Cannon to do the scan today. They didn't sedate him and he was petrified. He cried and tears rolled down his face and we couldn't do it as he had to be still. So, we need to try again tomorrow. My heart just aches for him! I wipe tears from his eyes so many times a day and I say, "Mummy here, no cry, buddy. It's okay! Mumma here." He cries when we do mouth care three times a day, when I bathe him with these horrific wipes, when I take him out of bed, when I moisturize him. It never ends, all day long. He is so fed up now. I just want to pick him up and walk out the front door with him and pretend he doesn't have cancer.

I have read many poems saying, "cancer can't do this, cancer can't do that", and that's all great and flowery and poetic, so to speak, but it's not reality.

This is the reality:

cancer has taken over our lives
cancer has my family living in two cities

But more than that...

cancer has taken my son's smile
cancer has taken my son's laugh
cancer has taken my son's appetite
cancer has taken his spunk
cancer has taken his patience
cancer has taken his hair
cancer has burned his skin off
cancer put him through a thirteen hour surgery
cancer has made him basically live in a hospital for six months
cancer has stolen so much from my son!!

I say all this because I want all who read this to take action! As one little girl, Gabriella Miller, said in the Truth365 video, and I'm quoting here, "Talk is bullshit. We need action."

Things need to change for these kids! I promise, if you lived one day in this crazy cancer world you would understand, but I can't show you that, nor do I wish that on anyone. So please, take me at my word. Can you do that? Take me at my word! Tell one person about kids' cancer and the lack of funding! St. Baldrick's and Alex's Lemonade Stand are wonderful places to donate. I encourage you to give up one gift you would have this year and place five bucks with one of these charities. They only fund kids' cancer research! I know many cancers need help and I support those, but these kids are so underfunded. Take my word for it, please. They deserve better and I believe, together, we can do this! I have failed these kids, as many of us have. You and I were unaware before. Now we are aware! We need action!!

Please hug your kids longer, read to them longer, make bedtime just a little later, give them a little extra treat and, above all, every single day kiss and cuddle them and tell them how proud you are and how you love them so! Life can be short and the train can hit at any time, day or night. Live life with gratitude for all things, small and big!

Food For The Soul
Written Nov 13, 2013 5:24pm

It is difficult in words for me to explain the joy in my heart when Cannon smiles or feels good, but I will try. My insides change, they loosen up. It doesn't feel like I am being punched over and over or doing a million sit ups. My stomach relaxes, I get an appetite and my shoulders stop tensing. My heart feels like it begins to mend.

This morning Cannon woke up at 2am and I didn't get him back to sleep until 7:30am. He stood up in his bed (first time since transplant) and signed to get out of bed. So, out of the bed he came and sat on the chair. I went to the bathroom and when I came out and he was off the chair and climbing over my blow up bed. I couldn't believe my eyes. Where did his strength come from? I was shocked after the past two days. He then, with my help, walked to the door. It is now 4:45am and we walked to the playroom. I was in shock, frankly. Cannon played with toys and then he wobbled back to our room.

The air in Cannon's room and in the halls in the transplant area is filtered to help these kids stay healthy since their immune systems are so suppressed. Cannon must also wear a mask which, by the way, he only did for the first time this morning. That's how much he wanted out of the room. My baby is growing up.

Tomorrow Cannon will have an NG tube placed. The tube goes down his nose into his stomach and will be used to feed him. Sadly, we have failed at feeding and hydrating him. Michael and I have done a lot of research and spoken with many families and decided it's for the best. It was not and is NOT an easy decision for us as Cannon's parents. As a mother, to not be able to feed my child feels like I failed. It's very sad, but very necessary. I just need to put on my big girl pants and be there for Cannon tomorrow.

Cannon has a long way to go, but today was one step forward and no steps back. I will take it!!! Thankful for small blessings.

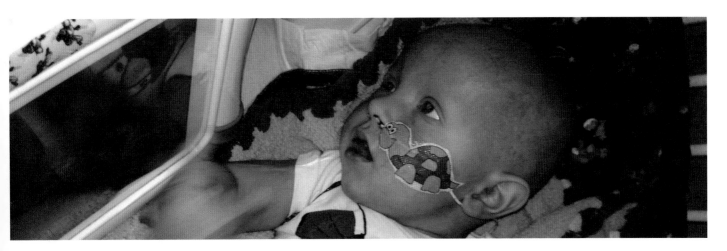

"It's Okay, Mumma Here"
Written Nov 19, 2013 9:48pm

Last night was a bit of a rough night, which you would know if you could see the black bags under my eyes. Cannon was sick at 10pm, 12am and 6am. He appeared really agitated and sore.

It's sad to me to see how much Cannon has had to grow up during this process. It hurts my heart. He was a baby, and seven months later, he seems like a little boy.

Today, I wheeled Cannon away in a wheelchair for him to be put under for his CT simulation in preparation for his radiation. The whole way, he was anxious, nervous, looking around, shaking. My heart just broke over and over and over! It's so sad... he is just two years old. He is really aware of what's going on as this process progresses. I almost wish he was younger or older and not this age. I know no age is easy, I just hate that I can't talk to him, or should I say, that he can't talk back to me. I rub his back and I say, "It's okay, Mumma here", but it never seems enough. If I could give my life today for Cannon, and give him a healthy one, I would - but I can't!

As we were wheeled out of the isolation floor to another hospital for the first time, Cannon signed to me for trees and grass and to go outside! It crushed me. He has been inside for five weeks, primarily in a tiny room, and has had little contact with anyone but nurses and doctors! Roll on discharge!!!

Tomorrow we will do the MIBG/CT and line removal. Pray hard for clear scans!

Did I Say This Already? NED, NED!

Written Nov 21, 2013 4:08am

It's 4am and I literally feel like I am twelve years old again and Santa is coming in the morning.

I have not been this happy since the day they placed Cannon in my arms twenty-seven months ago and said you can feed him now. That I did. He ate like a champ, too! My life was changed forever that day! I was twenty-seven and had wanted to carry a child and be a mumma for so long. It is something I truly never took for granted because I know how hard so many couples try to have babies, or want babies, and they don't get that blessing. I have never taken that for granted! Today I had that same JOY!!!!!!!

It was an intense day. We were taken to the scan area in nuclear medicine at 11:30am. At around 1:30pm, after much sweet-talking (I think it was my Scottish brogue), the radiologist said, "You can stand here and take a peek at the screen if you'd like." Some lady was all bent out of shape asking, "Why is the family in here?" I just walked right past her to the screen like she didn't exist (as my dad says, "There is always one Mel, there is always one." LOL). On the screen there was nothing lit up on the scan (areas of concern light up). I have seen every scan Cannon has ever had on the screen (thank you, APH) and so I knew this scan looked different but honestly, I couldn't process it. I didn't want to get my hopes up. The radiologist said, "The doctor will explain, but we will not do a CT fuse today." In my mind I'm like, "That has to be a good sign, right?" Of course, Nicole and I, and Dad in Orlando, over-analyzed her response for the rest of the day!!!

By 4:30pm, Cannon was done in recovery and we went back to isolation. The next one and a half hours were literally as bad as waiting for Cannon in surgery. Nicole and I were just pacing around the room. I, of course, asked the nurse about ten times if the results were back. Around 5:45pm, they said "They are working on them and the results will be ready in a couple of minutes." If you tell me a couple of minutes, I think one, two, three, maybe even five... but, fourteen minutes (yes, fourteen) go by and the doctor walked in and said, "All negative, there is nothing on the scan!" I said, "Ok, hold on, Cannon is NED?" and she said, "Yes, he is." Wooo hooooooooo!!!!! Nicole and I high-fived and were shown the images on a computer.

I quickly called Michael and said, "NED, Baby! NED!" He said, "No." I said, "Yes, sir." The phone went silent. "Are you there?" He was crying, just such joy - pure joy!!!!!! We cried together and we rejoiced! It was just joyful!!!! November 20, 2013... I will never forget that day! Never!!!

It really doesn't change anything about Cannon's treatment, except we need to decide if we will radiate his leg (we don't need to decide today).

Today, day thirty-seven (six weeks to the day since Cannon and I came to Philly), we will get on a private plane to Orlando using air time donated to us by Corporate Angels. We will be home for ten days and then back to Philly! Can you see my smile? I am doing a happy dance. It ain't pretty but it's all I got, people!

Cannon still isn't eating or drinking anything! I just know as soon as I sit him on his sofa today he will be a different kid! He is beyond over it now! He cries every time the door opens and someone comes in and touches him. He is also withdrawing badly from the pain meds and having a hard time with that, but as I always say...

Slow and steady wins the race!!

It's Not Over... What Does NED Mean?
Written Nov 23, 2013 5:00pm

A lot of people have asked me if Cannon is done with treatment since the scan showed no evidence of disease...

I wish!!!!!!!

Neuroblastoma kills more kids five years of age and under than any other cancer or disease in the world. So although the scan shows no disease, it doesn't mean there are not cancer cells still lurking. One cell can turn into millions very quickly with this disease.

Cannon has a gene called N-Myc amplified, which means his tumor was tested and it's, well, as one oncologist said, "a nail in the coffin." It basically means his tumors are very fast-growing and are harder to kill than those that are not amplified.

That's the long way of saying we are not even halfway through Cannon's treatment. Cannon will undergo radiation for the month of December. In January, he will begin antibodies for six months, which is done in the ICU. It's very painful, but very effective!!! Then he will take oral pills for six months (the easy part). So I wish, wish, wish I could say, "Yes, it's all over." But, it's kind of like running a marathon and you are told you did great and you can finish early, but you would not really be done and you wouldn't get your medal unless you went all the way to the finish line. Well, Cannon is only seven miles into the marathon and has a long road to go. He is doing awesome and fighting so hard, but he still has a long road to go! We want Cannon to get the medal, so we must go all the way to the end so he can be cancer-free for life!!!

Cannon is happy to be home but, I won't lie, it's still stressful. It's just a different stress. Cannon is in a lot of pain, he is withdrawing from the pain meds, he is shaking and achy like he has the flu. He hasn't walked around hardly at all. He just sits and doesn't want to be touched. He still won't eat and drink. He is on a lot of meds every four hours. I really do admire the nurses who do this for three patients a night. It's kind of amazing!!

December 4th 2013

230 DAYS

SINCE DIAGNOSIS

The survival rate for most forms of childhood cancer have stagnated (not increased) in the last 30 years, due primarily to gaps in crucial research funding.

*Source: BandofParents.org

Hard Decisions: Eight Months Since Diagnosis
Written Dec 4, 2013 7:11am

Cannon and I are back in Philly after ten days at home.

We are almost eight months into Cannon's aggressive treatment and everyone is just exhausted. Cannon is beyond done with it all. I honestly thought this process could not get any more difficult or challenging, but it has and does. Cannon is still not eating. In almost seven weeks he has had some popcorn, a bite of hashbrown, some apple juice and a little protein shake. The NG tube continues to be his source for feeds. This makes me very sad.

In the spirit of honesty and openness, I confess it was harder being home in Orlando than we anticipated. Cannon was really hard work as he was just having such a hard time withdrawing from the pain meds. He has been in such pain that I took him to CHOP today. Dr. Grupp decided to up the meds because he doesn't want Cannon in pain. It makes me sad to up the meds when we worked so hard to get them down, but Cannon is just not doing well with the reduction and has basically been so miserable most days. Today we upped one of the doses and Cannon played longer and harder than I have seen since we weaned him down. It hurt my heart. You constantly question all you do as a mother, regardless of whether your child is sick or not. But in this situation, you constantly wonder, "Am I doing enough? Is this right? What else can I do?" I beat myself up about how I had weaned Cannon off the meds too soon and how he had this pain of withdrawal unnecessarily. I do have these days where I just miss our old life: the carefree days of Cannon and I enjoying days out, and giggles and laughs. No looming hospital trips, travel to hospitals or huge life-changing decisions. It was the best twenty months of my life. Until April 19, 2013, when our lives changed FOREVER!

Talking about decisions - Michael and I did decide on Cannon's leg. I can say this was one of the hardest decisions of our life. After lots of research, prayer, and communication with many doctors, all of whom had different opinions, Michael and I went to dinner to decide on what to do. We both took time apart before dinner and processed what we thought was best for Cannon. I was a little nervous we would have decided differently, and I was ready to go to battle for my choice. However, I didn't want to. I wanted us to be on the same page. At the same time we both said, "I don't want to radiate the leg." I am so thankful we both felt the same way. We have been on the same page the entire process and I'm thankful we continue to be. We will radiate Cannon's chest all the way down to his diaper area. It's a large area and a lot of toxins for his body. Side effects long-term are lack of growth in the spine area. Most kids make it to five feet, or five feet, two inches, if they're lucky. I don't care what height my son is, but I know someday he will. It is then I will explain to him that he is lucky to be alive. Just like my dad used to tell my sister when she complained of back pain, "You're lucky you're walking, so stop complaining." Love that guy - cruel to be kind!

Naptime = Update Time
Written Dec 7, 2013 3:05pm

All three boys are napping, so I can take a minute and update everyone. My updates are less frequent as I am one busy Mumma and I love, love, love it and I live, live, live for them!

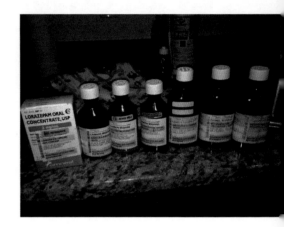

Cannon had a really rough week. We were meant to start proton radiation on Thursday but instead we found ourselves back at CHOP. We will now start radiation on Monday. So, we will be in Philly for Christmas, but that's okay. I couldn't care less where we are, so long as we're together. And Daddy Wiggins and I decided Christmas this year will be the 27th of December, when we get home.

I think we have the pain issue for Cannon under control now. We believe he was having a blockage issue and have been prescribed meds to help. We have seen an amazing transformation since yesterday. So great... Cannon ate one and a half chicken nuggets and a bite of hashbrown over the last two days (more than the last seven weeks!). We are just thrilled as it means he is starting to feel hungry! What a gift! He is moving around better and smiling more and, well, can you feel it? Can you hear it? That's called a Scottish mumma's happy heart.

Radiation: Children's Hospital of Philadelphia -- Pennsylvania
Written Dec 9, 2013 6:31pm

Today Cannon will begin proton radiation from the top of his chest bone to his diaper area. The entire area will be radiated and the most obvious thing, and the thing we know for certain, is his spine won't grow in areas, which will result in Cannon being around five feet tall. Who cares as long as he is alive, right? The other issue is that radiation can cause secondary cancers, and children with neuroblastoma have a higher chance of secondary cancers due to the high toxin levels they receive from their treatment. One day and one challenge at a time, I say!

The great news is that neuroblastoma is very sensitive to radiation, so it's deemed a very effective treatment if you have minimal disease. Cannon would fall into that realm as he is NED. I have to say, I do love typing that word!!! And I pray, no relapse EVER!!!

If I Had A Wish
Written Dec 16, 2013 12:38pm

If I had a wish...

It would be that ALL cancer didn't exist...

If I couldn't be granted that wish, I would wish cancer in kids didn't exist...

If I couldn't be granted that wish, I would wish that my son was healthy and happy...

"I would wish that my son was healthy and happy…"

If I could have no wishes, I would FIGHT. I would fight until my dying day on this earth. I will fight for ALL the kids. Some think this is all about Cannon and, if you do, you don't know me. Yes, it's true, this STARTED with Cannon, but the fighting I do is for ALL the kids. I have, we have, team Cannonball has BIG plans on how to fight this beast, how to create awareness, how to get blood donations and how to beat the CRAP out of all kids' cancer.

Yes, it's true, Cannon is where this started, but he is NOT where this story will end!! I am in this now, and I am in this all my days. It's in my soul. It's my mission, my life. No matter where my son's story ends... this is only the beginning.

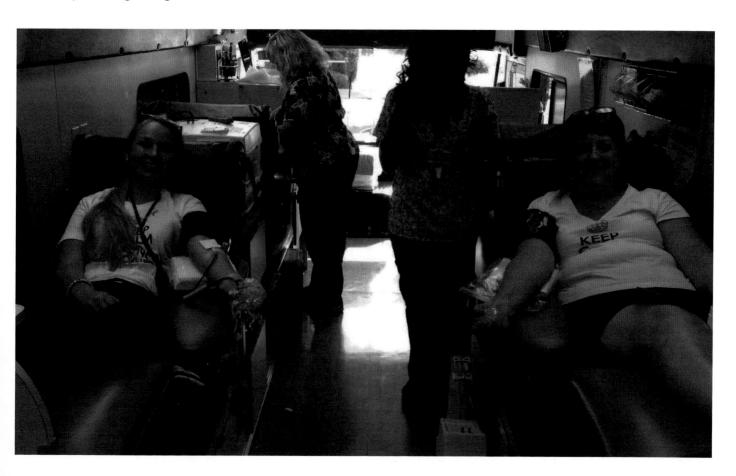

Happening FOR Us Not TO Us
Written Dec 19, 2013 3:43pm

Interesting... right?

What if things in life happen FOR us, not TO us?

What if Cannon having cancer happened so we are able to have the strength to fight for all the kids that need better treatments, more funding?

I am not wise enough to think of that myself, but a friend said it to me. "This is being done FOR you, not TO you."

I love that type of thinking. I have always been, and continue to be, the person who believes there is, and must be, a positive out of every outcome, good or bad.

I know if I were a truly humble person I would say, "God, I know you may want to take Cannon and I know you know best." Believe me, I try. But I can't find it in me to say those words, and I don't. However, I do believe everything happens for a reason. I do believe Cannonball Kids' cancer has a purpose in this world and I do believe Cannon will make it out of this alive.

Merry Christmas From Cannon And Mumma-Bear

Written Dec 25, 2013 2:11pm

Michael, Olivia, Nicole and the twins are in Orlando. They left earlier this morning.

It was beyond painful to pack all morning and kiss my babies goodbye... all of them. You included, Dada Wiggins. This morning when I woke up, I had tears in my eyes when I looked at the monitor to see the twins. No newborn should be without their Mumma-Bear, especially at Christmas. No family should be apart, ever, let alone at Christmas. I hope we can celebrate when Cannon and I get home, but I'm not sure it will quite feel the same.

Cannon and I have hardly been home since July due to surgery in New York, stem cell in Philly and then radiation also here in Philly. We have hardly been home in five months. We both can't wait to be home and to finish all our treatment in Orlando at the place we love the most, Arnold Palmer Hospital for Children. Oh, and I heard there is a new train!

On a nice, exciting note, Cannon has some eyelashes, eyebrows and hair coming in. That is very exciting! I miss styling his mohawk. In fact, can you imagine when I can do three mohawks? I can't wait!

Radiation - CHECK
Written Dec 27, 2013 2:05pm

It's really over, woo hooo!! The last radiation treatment is done and we can check another step off our list.

As I sit here typing on the sofa, Cannon is beside me and seems most pleased with himself. I have always said and still believe that he understands much more than we give him credit for.

I am very excited. Tomorrow we fly home after living away from home almost completely since July.

Antibody treatment starts in the Intensive Care Unit at APHC on January 19. But today I don't need to think about it. Instead, I choose to rejoice in the fact that Cannonball did it! He really did it!!!

January 8th 2014
265 DAYS
SINCE DIAGNOSIS

Pharmaceutical companies fund over
50% of adult cancer research,
but less than 5% for children's cancer
research.

Source: SolvingKidsCancer.org

Naïve No More... The Truth About neuroblastoma

Written Jan 8, 2014 2:01pm

Cannon and I are home now and all three boys are taking a nap, so I'm sitting down and wanted to take a minute and update you all.

Cannon's bone marrow biopsy was done this morning and we should get results potentially tomorrow or Friday.

Antibody treatment is really most effective if the patient has no cancer showing in the scans and the bone marrow.

Naïve no more...

Recently I read a study which was taken of 343 patients with stage four neuroblastoma, whose disease had spread from the primary tumor and who were at least eighteen months old, like Cannon. Of those who still had minimal residual disease in their bone marrow (i.e. even a tiny cell of cancer, no matter how small) after two cycles of antibodies, ALL 343 patients relapsed and died within five years.

So when I say I get anxious about these bone marrow test results and what they will say, it's not just because I think this is scary. It's because if there is disease showing in the test and, if I believe in the studies I read, then my son will die.

My son will die? I feel like I could be sick at any moment thinking that thought, but that's the reality of stage four neuroblastoma. No one wants to think it, say it, dream it, believe it - none of it. But, I am not naïve, I'm very realistic to what these tests can do to change our lives forever... beyond what we have experienced to-date, which seems impossible. But believe me, it's true.

So when I say I feel anxious, what I mean is this: I'm scared. I'm really, really scared my son could die. I am terrified these could be my last days with him. Does that make me negative? No, I don't believe so. Does that make me lack faith? I don't think so. Does that render me hopeless? Not in my opinion. But it does make me realistic. I am naïve no more.

I was naïve to the truth before living in this kids' cancer world. I was even naïve when we began this journey. But then I witnessed kid after kid after kid go to Heaven. Well, slowly the cancer eats away at your naïvety of it all and, slowly but surely, you begin to think, "Could my son be next?" Well, could he?

I feel like I walk around with a big bag of coal on my back every day; an elephant on my chest and a knife in my heart. Today we were only at the hospital for five hours and I feel like I ran a marathon.

Watching Cannon be put under yet again, watching him be drilled into… it is just exhausting mentally to watch him suffer over and over and over and never catch a break. Next week we start antibodies and I feel like I could just scoop all my boys up and hop on a plane to Scotland and never come back. I wish I could escape with my family healthy and happy.

Of course, the reality is we will stick to the course. Albeit painful to endure, it's saving our son's life.

Not NED, Not cancer-Free, But It Will Be Okay

Written Jan 16, 2014 3:31pm

"Rehearsing your troubles results in experiencing them many times. You are meant to go through them only once. Do not multiply your suffering."

~ Jesus Calling, Sarah Young

I am utilizing that today. I won't think of relapse today, or that Cannon may not beat this awful disease, or of living my life without him. I will, just for today, not rehearse my troubles. Instead, I will smile, be goofy with my kids and live for their laughter, for laughter is truly the best medicine of all.

Cannon's urine test levels were not at a normal level. What does this mean? It means he is not NED, it means he is not cancer-free. But it will be okay.

I have had a day to process the news and this is my view: We went into stem cell with Cannon's knee still having the cancer. Stem cell transplant got rid of the cancer in his leg. Antibodies or immunotherapy will get rid of those pesky nb cells that remain in his body. Period!

It would have been more difficult going into antibodies with Cannon being NED because it's hard to fathom why we have to put him through this if he is cancer-free. Would I prefer he is cancer-free? Of course, BUT this test result means there is no choice. We cannot stop at this point even if we wanted to because the cancer remains in his body and it grows at lightning speed. So, in a kind of sick, twisted way, I want antibodies to start like yesterday, because every day we wait those tiny cells grow, and grow, and grow, and if you leave them too long they cannot be contained or stopped.

Today in the education class for antibody treatment, the instructor said, „I'm sorry he has to go through this… it's going to be hard." I responded, „I'm thankful that antibodies exist and that Cannon has the best chance possible to beat this horrific cancer." Truly, that's how I feel. Five years ago this treatment didn't exist and the addition of this treatment has made survival rates go from twenty percent to fifty percent. So yes, it will be hard, but I also believe it will be extremely effective.

As I drove home, I used the automatic window button and put Cannon's window up and down, over and over again (you know how kids love repetition). He belly laughed over and over. Sometimes when he is that happy, I find my heart aching as now, after my education class, I know what's coming. I know the horror he will face as of Monday. I know I'm going to have to listen to Cannon scream and cry in pain and look at me to help him… and I can't.

Antibody is, I'm told, the most painful treatment of all. How is that possible? But, it is.

Cannon can do this, but it shouldn't be this hard…

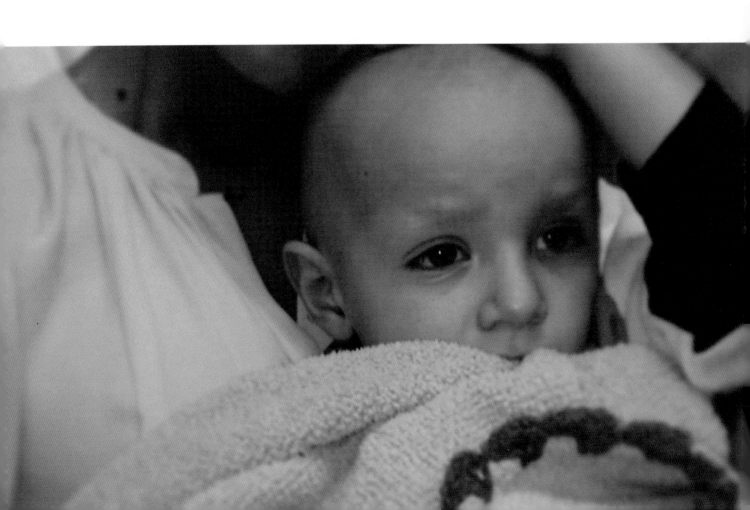

Preparing For Antibodies - Blog By Dad, Michael Wiggins
Written Jan 18, 2014 11:35am

So, we move forward. I will drive Cannon to APHC on Sunday night to admit him with that miserable hole-in-my-stomach feeling. I know what his reaction will be when I put him in the stroller to go up to the fourth floor room for the week - crying and that look to me of, "Why, Dad?"

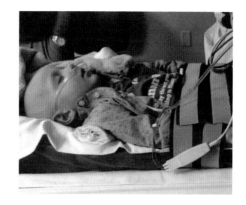

The problem with antibody therapy, and despite all the potential side effects, the one Melissa and I dread the most for Cannon, is pain. Put simply, the therapy is known to be very painful to the kids, and pre-dosing and pre-medicating with morphine or stronger drugs and monitoring for more, is standard and expected. Quite frankly, I am tired of watching my child suffer in pain, and I absolutely hate for him the thought that we face the next six months of knowing we are pushing Cannon forward to cure him, but have to push him through hell to do it. One neuroblastoma parent told me this about immunotherapy: "It's like watching your kid get electrocuted several times throughout the day." Pains my heart for Cannon.

The good news? In six months, Cannon will be cancer-free and through the treatment protocol for neuroblastoma, and we will put this, chemo, surgery, stem cell transplant, radiation and all of it in our rear-view mirror and watch him grow up to be the little boy God intended for our family.

Baptism Yesterday... ICU Today
Written Jan 20, 2014 8:51am

Have you ever had one of those days where you look around you and just feel so good? Yesterday, I had my husband, my three boys and so many amazing friends around me.

My angels were baptized. Yes, in their kilts. ;)

Getting three boys in kilt attire and out of the house by 8am was a challenge, but one I relish. I truly believe I was put on this planet to be a mother... the greatest gift in the world. Nothing can ever compare to how I feel about being a mother.

Right now, I sit in the Intensive Care Unit with Cannon. I just held him down to get his IV placed and the nightmare begins. The tears flowing, his mood changing. I am clock watching... his infusion begins at 10am. We are told things will get hairy around noon, two hours after the infusion of the antibody begins. It feels like I'm standing on a railroad track and I'm waiting for the train to hit me, but I'm not sure how painful it will be. I just know it will be. I don't know exactly when the train will arrive but I know it's around noon. My stomach hurts as I hold my baby and cuddle him in bed. He was a happy smiley boy yesterday and now he is crying and sad.

This is what I have to say to you, neuroblastoma: You may have started the marathon ten miles ahead of us, but we caught up and now we have six miles to go and you're only a mile ahead of us. Watch your back. We are fast finishers and we hate losing! Winners never quit, quitters never win! We are winners, neuroblastoma, and I'm saying this confidently, no matter how hard this marathon is, no matter the toll on Cannon's body, he will win. For he is a winner!

Day One Of Immunotherapy Antibodies: Nine Months Since Diagnosis
Written Jan 21, 2014 7:30am

Cannon has been in this race for nine months now and it's been a lot for my angel but, I've said it before, Cannon is something special. He is not typical for his age. Exhibit A: Yesterday as Cannon was in excruciating pain he closed his eyes and tried to mentally go inward and manage his pain. It is hard to explain, but it was like he was meditating. It was like he was trying to convince himself, "You've got this Cannon, it's okay." I lay beside him the entire day just in awe of his strength. He is two, and he has spent the last nine months in hospitals fighting for his life.

I have said it before, but I'm so thankful for the antibodies. Neuroblastoma is notorious for coming back and there is no cure for it. In fact, we're told kids have a three to five percent survival rate with relapse. It terrifies me that Cannon still has live cancer cells in his body; that he really was never NED. Cannon has not relapsed. His scans show no disease, but his urine shows disease. The urine should be normal after all the treatment Cannon has completed. It's kind of insane to think it could survive with all his little 30 pound body has endured. The urine showing disease means the cancer still lives in his body, and neuroblastoma is rapid growing, so to say I am thankful for the antibodies doesn't do my feelings justice.

Hurts My Heart
Written Jan 23, 2014 10:00am

This morning Cannon was pointing to the corner of the room and was very frustrated with me as I kept bringing things to which I thought he was pointing.

What was he pointing at? A pink bucket he knows is for when he is sick. I brought it over and he leaned his head over it to vomit. I'm choked-up as I type this. He is two, and he knows to vomit in the pink bucket. He pulled me in really close to him and I got in bed and rubbed his back.

I don't want my baby to grow up. What parent does, right? Oh, you know I'll be the mother-in-law from hell. I can see it now... "My Mum wants to come for dinner" and the wife saying, "Again?" LOL :)

But what I really don't want is my kid to grow up in the hospital, and that's what's happening. How does my son know the pink bucket is for being sick? How does he know to not pull out the IV that's in his arm or pull out the oxygen in his nose? Well, simply, because this is where he has grown up.

I am going to share something I'm ashamed to say, but I think maybe it will help other mums in this position, so I will share. Last night, I was cleaning up Cannon's room and I sat beside one of his blankets and my mind said, "Keep that aside, then at least you can smell it if Cannon doesn't make it." It was an awful thought, and as soon as my brain went there, I said, "No - he will make it." I confess, sometimes my brain goes there and, as soon as it does, I tell myself, "No!!!!" To imagine life without Cannon... well, it's not life at all. It will be existing, for he is my everything. He is a very important part of my puzzle, just like my husband, Olivia and my twins.

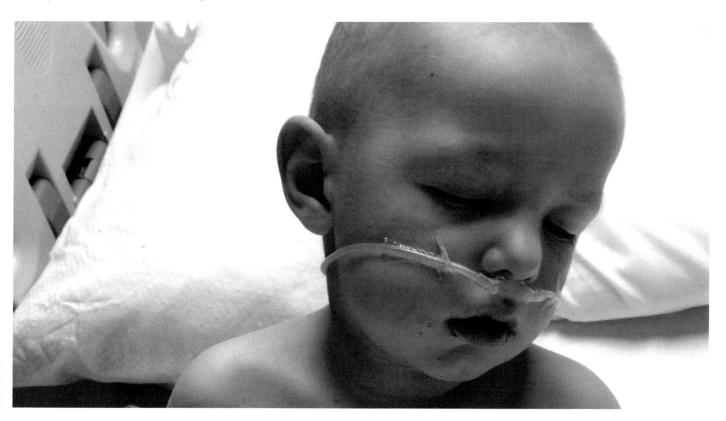

February 3rd 2014

291 DAYS

SINCE DIAGNOSIS

So severe is the pain and misery and the
suffering of children who undergo treatment
for cancer, that the suffering would be
considered impermissible torture pursuant to
the United Nations Convention Against Torture
if inflicted on an adult as punishment.

*Source: Kidsvcancer.org

This Marathon Is Hard, But We Must Finish

Written Feb 3, 2014 2:11pm

Sunday is fast approaching and I am trying my hardest to not think about it, but it seems to pop into my head on every occasion. On Sunday we will go inpatient for two weeks. I will stay in the hospital and not get to tuck in my twin baby boys. My heart is breaking.

All I can say is, right now, my son is not living! He is in pain daily, he is so weak he falls over, he is gray in color, he is so skinny his bones stick out, he doesn't want to play or run around, despite my trying EVERYTHING known to man to make him feel better, to make him smile, to make him feel happy. He isn't a regular kid and hasn't been since April 19, 2013. The pain to watch him be tortured to save his life is beyond anything I could say here. It's torture... pure torture.

As we save his life, he continues to fall behind developmentally and physically. I watch other kids his age run around, jump on things and talk to their parents and my heart aches. I've never heard my son talk or watched him go up the steps to a slide on his own. Why? Because cancer riddled his legs and body, and he is weak. The chemo has weakened his mouth muscles, delaying his speech. The treatment these kids endure is nothing less than pure torture.

I feel like my family is living in hell. How I miss the real smiles on my face and the lightness in my mood and heart. I'm heavy. I'm really heavy, and my heart feels like it shatters every time Cannon cries, which is often.

I wish I had a positive post. I wish I could say Cannon was great. I wish a lot of things were different.

We didn't ask for this challenge. I wish this cancer had been given to me and not my son.

I want so badly to stop the treatment and be done, but I know we must finish this marathon... no matter the pain. And, like a marathon, as the miles go on you get more and more tired, and as the miles go on you get more pain. But in order to win, you must finish. In order to get a medal, you must finish. Cannon must cross the finish line, and as his mother, I intend to help him do that, no matter the pain!! Cannon deserves a medal and I will make sure he gets it!

We Have No Answers

Written Feb 4, 2014 9:07pm

Cannon has not been doing well. His weight before antibodies was around thirty-one pounds, and today he was twenty-six pounds. He is so frail the skin sags around his arms and every rib and bone in his body can be seen. My 9-month-old twin boys are only six pounds lighter than him. It's gut-wrenching. His port is sticking out so much I have to be careful when I lift him. I am so gentle with him because he is so frail.

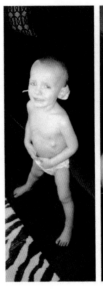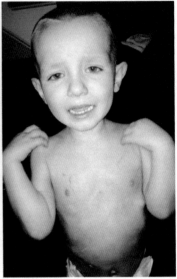

Today I had the three boys with me and we took Cannon for X-rays because they thought he had pneumonia. When the doctor listened to his lungs they were crackly all over. The scans looked fine; the doctor suspects it's viral. Due to his severely suppressed immune system, Cannon can't fight anything. We are monitoring him very carefully.

The week of antibodies was a walk in the park compared to what it's been like since we left the hospital. And now, on Sunday, I need to take him back in his condition for two more weeks of it? Do you ever get that horrible feeling when you can't take a proper breath in your chest? I have had that feeling constantly this past week.

The twins are so happy and healthy and I almost feel guilty when I laugh with them because Cannon is so incredibly miserable and sad. It's just heartbreaking.

Michael and I are so tired of seeing Cannon so miserable. The hardest part for me, as a mother, is the helplessness I feel. I am supposed to protect my babies and make sure no harm comes to them until the day I die, yet daily, I feel I fail my son. I fail him because I can't stop his tears and pain.

"Thank you, Prayer Warriors... thank you!"

I want to share this because a problem shared is a problem halved. This past week has been one of the scariest weeks for me as a mother, thus far. How can that be, you say? I have had this pain in my chest all week, this feeling of real uneasiness, real pain and discomfort that something bad was happening with Cannon. I have not slept much and neither has my husband.

You know you should never ask a question unless you are ready for the answer. I remember asking the doctor who diagnosed Cannon, "Is he going to die?" I fully expected, "No, of course not, we just have to do some chemo and he will be fine." That wasn't the response I was given. Instead, it went more like this: "He has a fight on his hands and it's fifty-fifty on whether he will make it or not." Of course at that point, I didn't know what I know now.

This week, for the first time, I have feared Cannon's life was coming to an end. The rapid weight loss, the non-stop cries of distress, the viral pneumonia that the doctor confirmed, the not eating and drinking. He acted as though he really didn't want to be alive. I literally tried everything to make him happy... distracting him, feeding him... you name it, I tried it, all while my insides were screaming, "Please don't die!"

I FELT LIKE WE WERE BUYING TIME...

I don't know what you prayer warriors did, but I know this: today Cannon STOOD, yes STOOD, at the train! Today he giggled! Today he smiled! Something changed overnight. I don't know what, but it did. He hasn't eaten so we will go back on the NG tube on Sunday when we go inpatient. Cannon is far from back to normal as he battles the viral pneumonia, but he is on the RISE, if today is anything to go by.

THANK YOU, PRAYER WARRIORS... THANK YOU!

We are going to keep a VERY close eye on Cannon and his pneumonia. We're told this next round of antibodies starting today will be the hardest, rounds two and four, that is. There can be some real breathing issues with this round. Cannon already having pneumonia makes it concerning to the doctor. Thankfully we will be in the ICU, which at APHC is incredible and they will really take care of us.

Mumma-Bear Request, Round Two Antibody Therapy

Written Feb 16, 2014 2:55pm

Can I ask for prayers as we head into round two of antibodies? The end is in sight with only six rounds of antibodies left and July 15 is getting closer, yet it still seems so far.

I sit on my front porch and the sun is shining... your typical seventy degree February weather in Orlando. Sorry Pennsylvania warriors! I look at the baby monitor showing all my boys happy and content, everyone napping including Dada Wiggins and Olivia, and the house is so peaceful. Yet I don't feel peace; I feel a knot in my stomach. Today at church, the priest spoke about peace and how peace was freedom. Well, I'm chained up in the bondage of self. I am not at peace with what my son suffers daily.

" Round two and four are the hardest. Kids have a lot of breathing issues in round two. Round two is horrific. Next week is the hard week."

I want so badly to sit down, chill out, and enjoy the day, but it is becoming near impossible. I appreciate I shouldn't mentally torture myself for what tomorrow brings but, somehow, I always end up there. Perhaps I need to try harder.

The words ring in my ear, "Round two and four are the hardest. Kids have a lot of breathing issues in round two. Round two is horrific. Next week is the hard week."

So I am at your mercy, again, and I ask for prayers for Cannon... that his pain is minimal and he can finally become NED.

They took urine from Cannon again last week and still the cancer lives in him, and so my baby has never been NED. I confess like I always do, this terrifies me. How, after six rounds of chemo, three surgeries including a thirteen hour tumor resection, twelve doses of radiation, a stem cell transplant and a round of antibodies, can cancer POSSIBLY still live in his body?

As you get closer to the finish line in this race, other fears set in, like the "R" word no one ever wants to hear... relapse. In this type of cancer, stage four neuroblastoma, there is no cure for relapse. The survival percentage is two to five percent. Relapse is very, very common in neuroblastoma and our fear is always that we put Cannon through all of this and he relapses. I pray every day that's not his story, and I continue to believe, despite the fears that plague my mind and my day.

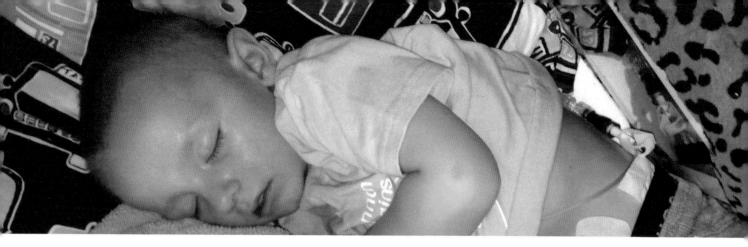

Prayers Needed Now... Antibody Complications
Written Feb 17, 2014 4:00pm

After a really rough start to the day, we had a few hours of peace.

However, Cannon has been having coughing spasms and, as a result, we have had to stop one of the drugs, the IL2. If he has any more spasms, we will stop the antibody.

This is very bad because he doesn't ever get to make it up. He just doesn't get to have it. No antibodies for any length of time is bad!

I went to the chapel and I got on my knees and I asked God to please intervene, please let him have these life-saving drugs. The cancer lives in him and without them he will die.

Please, God...

Antibody Stopped
Written Feb 18, 2014 1:18am

It's now 2am, and after another coughing spasm they won't run the antibody any longer.

The only way I can really describe it is like this: you know when your kid is choking on a piece of food and their face looks colorless and they look like they can't breathe? That's what these spasms look like. Cannon has the spasm and cries and looks at me to help and I can't help him.

The IL2 drug was stopped after only a few hours of infusing, and that's unfortunate because it basically helps the antibody fight and kill more cancer cells.

The antibody was shut off three and a half hours early.

With Cannon not being NED, it's terrifying - absolutely terrifying - not to mention the pain of watching him have these spasms.

To all the parents and grandparents who have had a kid with a runny nose, fever or short periods of sickness, you know how hard it is on your child. Imagine that feeling on steroids, and you can imagine a little of what's going on here. It's honestly why I am so driven to work tirelessly for these kids. I know many friends tell me to slow down, and I know I must sometimes, but that's beyond difficult when today and yesterday sixteen kids like Cannon died (eight per day), sixteen sets of parents and grandparents are suffering. So how can I slow down, stop, retract? I simply can't. Why? Cancer doesn't stop for anyone, so neither can I!

They are now giving Cannon a drug called hydrocortisone. The protocol discourages use of this drug as it can make the antibody less effective, but without it, the spasms won't stop.

Thank you to all who donate blood. From the bottom of my soul - thank you! Cannon will now receive packed red blood as his level is very low.

Ten Months On... It's Not Easier
Written Feb 19, 2014 11:09am

I looked at my phone today and realized it was the 19th... ten months we have been on this journey.

Our journey is not over and there is more to come. The date we know for sure is that antibodies will be finished and all scans completed by July 15, 2014. No matter what, they must be completed by then - per the protocol.

I truly believed the journey would get easier, and somehow seeing Cannon being put under, restrained, given blood transfusions, operated on, going through transplant, having to travel and being away from the twins would be... well, bearable at least. It's not.

Last night I spent the night with the twins and Arran James cried when he saw me and pulled me in tight as he could. He does it every time he is away from me. This morning at 7am, I kissed them goodbye knowing I would be in the hospital from now until Friday without seeing them and, well, it's not easier. It's not easier.

Olivia deserves to have someone there at the end of her school day to chat over her day, but often she doesn't. It's not how Michael and I want her last year at home before college to be. It's not easier.

The road to the end is closer, but it's not easier.

Sometimes I feel like I can't breathe, my chest is so tight and hurts so much.

This antibody treatment has brought so much fear. Not lack of faith, but fear into my heart. The problem is I know too much. I know too many families with kids who didn't receive antibodies, or all of the antibodies, and the kids relapsed or got a secondary cancer. Mothers are reaching out to me trying to help me because, like my fears, their fears are real and from experience.

Today they said they doubt Cannon will receive the antibody and tomorrow he may not either. I hate to put pressure on Cannon as I know he is over it, but I feel I inadvertently do. Like my husband said today, "We can't allow him to give up."

I can't tell you enough in words how I am trying so hard to, "Let go and let God", but when it comes to my baby boy that's almost impossible. I continue to strive to that place of peace.

Dear Cannon:

Your Mumma-Bear loves you more than life.

I am so sorry that I cannot protect you like I thought I could.

I am so sorry that cancer is taking away your early days which should be filled with nothing but fun and love.

I am so sorry that you sleep most nights not in your bedroom, which you love so much.

I am so sorry I can't take your place. I wish so badly I could.

I am so sorry that I didn't know something was wrong sooner so your prognosis was better.

I am sorry I had to leave you when you needed me to give birth to your brothers.

I am so sorry that, no matter what I do, I can't fix this, no matter how hard I try and how much it hurts to see you in pain.

I am so sorry I promised these antibodies would take the cancer away and now my promise is being broken to you.

I promise you this, baby boy: I will, until the day I die, make you proud of me. My actions to you and others will make you proud that I am your mother. I will help other kids with cancer like I know you want me to! I will be the mother you deserve.

I promise you, no matter what, I will never, ever, ever give up on you or this chance to save you!

The path may be rocky, and it may be hard, but you have Scottish-American blood in you. Nothing could be better.

Neuroblastoma may have stage four on its side, and it may be fierce, but nothing can defeat your heart. You are a warrior.

You are brave.
You are my Braveheart.
I will die fighting for you, son!
It's not over neuroblastoma. Keep coming at us. You may have won this fight but you won't win the war!

Love,
Mumma-Bear

Guess Who Is Receiving Antibodies?

Written Feb 19, 2014 6:17pm

After much negotiating, arm-bending, and persuading (politely), FINALLY the oncologist in charge agreed (even though he disagreed with me) to restart the antibody without the IL2. Cannon will only receive a portion of the antibody, but I will take all we can get.

I was told by the RN if we run into issues he will be intubated with a breathing tube down his throat. They wanted me to know all the risks of restarting it. I weighed the risks and to me it was the right choice.

So we started the antibody at 5:21pm and it will run for thirteen hours.

After we started it, Cannon woke up after sleeping the entire day and ate a huge bowl of pasta his Auntie Bridget fed him. It was awesome to see.

A Normal Family

Written Feb 27, 2014 5:32pm

Our little Cannonball, small in stature but big in heart, is progressing and doing better day-by-day. He is gaining weight. I weighed him today and he was twenty-eight pounds which is a two pound gain in just a week. Can I have high five on that one?

He has moments of happiness which are just beautiful. They are short but special to this Mumma-Bear. He is on medication which is part of the antibody study and it makes him kind of depressed and sad. For example, I will take the boys in the wagon and the twins smile, laugh, and sometimes steal toys from each other, and Cannon looks around but has no emotions... no smiles. I will point at wildlife and he gives me no interaction back. I know he is working so hard to fight the cancer but, boy-oh-boy, I miss my son. I know he will come back to me and this isn't about me, nor should it be, but when I get the glimpses of his happiness, I sure do miss that guy!

We have two weeks off and I know Cannon will get stronger and happier as we get closer to that admission date. I know I should live in the day, but I already have a pit in my stomach thinking about taking him back. My heart says, "Don't", but my head says, "He will die if you don't." Thankfully, I'm not a teenager anymore and can follow my head. ;) That said, I could never judge anyone who decided differently, as this journey is so painful. I am just so thankful I have my husband by my side. For the single parents, I pray... I pray hard.

I have to say, I sure have enjoyed the three boys all week. Many friends texted me to hang out and I didn't. I just wanted time with my boys by myself. I wanted my boys to get 100 percent of me because, well... the twins never get me and Cannon needs to learn he has siblings. There is just something in my heart that changes when I have all three of them with me... a peace. This week, just running errands like grocery shopping and going to the bank was fun because I had all of my boys with me. I honestly believe I was made to be a mum, it just comes naturally to me. It's not stressful (most of the time, LOL), it's a joy, a pleasure, especially when Cannon is feeling a little better. I pray he gets stronger and happier and we can make some family memories over the next two weeks we still have off.

March 11th 2014

327 DAYS

SINCE DIAGNOSIS

Childhood cancers are not related to
lifestyle factors,
and little can be done to prevent them.

*Source: St. Baldrick's

My Gift - Blog By Dad, Michael Wiggins
Written Mar 11, 2014 1:52pm

Yesterday was another birthday for Daddy and Cannon felt so strongly about celebrating that he woke up at 3:30am, got out of bed and starting playing... and never went back to bed! He has finally had enough time off between treatments to actually feel good and want to play, want to eat and want to smile. Melissa and I actually laughed at him and the crazy time of the morning because he walked out of the bedroom and into the nearly dark house and started pushing his truck around the kitchen and then back into the bedroom. So, because he was happy, and our hearts were happy for him, I got up with him and stayed up the rest of the morning and just played with him and let him watch his videos. He smiled, made all of his quirky happy noises, threw his giant bounce ball, all before 6am. Now that was a life gift to Dad. What a gift... I wouldn't ask for another thing.

Prayers Needed, Please
Written Mar 13, 2014 1:27pm

We went for a check-up this morning. There are a lot of things that must be checked before you start antibodies. We are due to start round three on Sunday.

Cannon was miserable at the hospital today, and as he started to feel better, well, he didn't want to be here AT ALL. He kept asking to leave and cried as we walked around trying to get his urine sample. Cannon isn't a crier so I knew something was up. As I lifted him from his stroller he seemed to be in a lot of pain.

Cannon has been having seizure-like episodes. They are so strange, his whole body tenses up and he shakes for a few seconds then it stops.

Today his liver enzyme levels were six hundred and seven hundred, and they need to be below forty in order to start the treatment on Sunday.

We will not start antibodies on Sunday. I don't know what this means yet.

You can imagine my being upset in not being able to have this life-saving treatment for Cannon.

I am struggling to watch Cannon so upset with being at the hospital and him not being able to have the antibodies. It's such an emotional roller coaster ride.

We are waiting to go for an ultrasound to see what's going on in case it is gallstones from all of his blood transfusions. Gallstones would require surgery. I'm praying it is not that, but also that it is not anything serious. He cannot eat or drink for four hours.

Please pray hard for my baby boy!

He needs this treatment, but first we have to figure out what is going on with his liver.

When Life Gives You Lemons: Eleven Months Since Diagnosis
Written Mar 14, 2014 7:43pm

When life gives you lemons - make lemonade...

Cannon and the twins were so happy all day - such a gift! My heart is so full of joy!

Tomorrow we have another fun-packed day at a St. Baldrick's event to help raise money for kids' cancer.

Cannon will not be admitted on Sunday. We pray he can start when his levels go down. That will be a minimum one week wait. Please pray Cannon's liver enzyme levels go down from seven hundred to forty so that we can continue to kill the neuroblastoma in his body.

Cannon is so happy and looks like a picture of health. He is really starting to gain strength. For the first time in his life he was able to go down steps at the park by himself. That might not sound like much to most mums of two-year-olds, but to this Mumma-Bear, well, it choked me up! Huge deal.

So instead of freaking out that Cannon can't have this treatment as planned, I'm making lemonade. We're doing daily speech, fattening Cannon up and showing him the time of his life. It's all fun in the Wiggins family now and I love it!

Thank You Team Cannonball Kids' cancer: Arnie's March, A Fundraiser For Arnold Palmer Hospital for Children's Oncology Team

Written Mar 18, 2014 8:41pm

Where do I start?

What a day...

I'm kind of lost for words. I know, right? A Scottish lassy lost for words? Truly though, I just don't know how to describe today and what it meant to me and our family to see everyone we love and care for supporting this incredible cause.

All I know is this: our incredible team raised $48,250, a total of thirty-three percent of the whole amount raised by all of the teams combined. I don't say that to brag, I promise. I say it because I am truly, truly in awe of the support for Team Cannonball - it just amazes me. Our team rocks!

Can I take a little moment to brag on my hubby? I am so proud of you, Michael Wiggins. There are many moments a woman can be proud of her husband, but watching my husband fight for all these kids, well, it gave me goosebumps. As Michael made his speech, Cannon just kept smiling at him and giggling – like, "Why is my dad up here talking to everyone?" Then he would run up to him and touch him and run back to me. It was so cute! Michael Wiggins, pediatric cancer did not know what it did when it hit on our son, our kids, our family, our life, our marriage. But I know this, Cannon will win this fight and we will continue fighting with all our might... for all of our lives. I couldn't think of a better teammate to fight with than you.

Thankful BUT Painful

Written Mar 24, 2014 3:04pm

Please don't think I am losing my gratitude for this fight. I am not... I could not. Just like I can be faithful but fearful, I can be thankful BUT it's still painful.

Last night, I don't think I've ever driven so slow to the hospital and trust me, I'm a speed-limit type of girl.

When we got to the hospital, Cannon was strangely happy. He was dancing on the spot and smiling and playing.

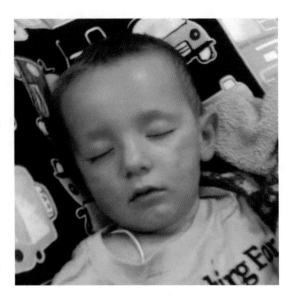

I am so thankful Cannon can start this treatment, but boy-oh-boy, it's painful as his mother to drive him to this life-saving treatment knowing everything we worked so hard for this last month (his longest break ever in treatment) - his speech, his strength, his diet, his weight, his HAPPINESS... it will all... GO!

Last night, I drove to the hospital with the happiest, healthiest form of my son I've seen in a year, maybe ever. Cannon was literally singing (his kind of singing), making noises and slapping his hands on his knees. It was beautiful.

As we started treatment this morning, that boy is gone. Cannon is screaming in pain and tears are running down his face.

It's so painful to watch. You begin to forget it's saving his life and become overwhelmed with the sadness in your child's eyes.

Cannon keeps pointing at his stroller and signing for us to leave and telling me he is all done - over and over again. I tell him I understand he wants to leave, but we can't right now. It's heartbreaking. I am a smart girl (most days) and I understand that this treatment is saving my son's life and we are getting closer to a cancer-free child, but man-oh-man, it's hard on my son. It's awful to watch.

I try to stay strong, and outwardly I do, but my chest is tight, my heart aches and my soul is sad.

I am so sorry, baby.

I am so sorry I have to make you sick to save you.

I am so sorry I can't take your pain.

I am so sorry I can't change this for you.

I am so sorry.

My heart aches for this sweet child I'm so privileged to call my son.

I'm so thankful for the fight, but it doesn't make it less painful.

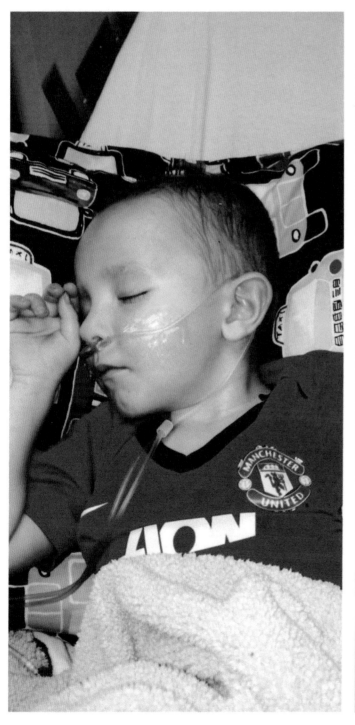

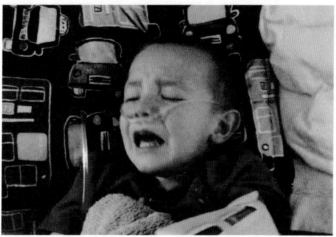

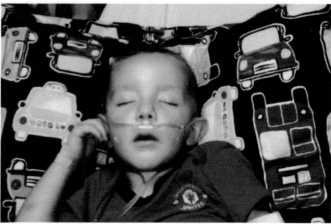

April 4th 2014

351 DAYS

SINCE DIAGNOSIS

Many adult cancers can be diagnosed early. In 80% of kids, cancer has already spread to other areas of the body by the time it is diagnosed.

*Source: St. Baldrick's

Beautiful Morning... Almost Normal... Almost

Written Apr 4, 2014 9:31am

Cannon and I did our usual routine (when not inpatient). We left at 7am and went to speech therapy. Watching Cannon improve in everything we do makes my heart happy. Cannon's therapist, Debra Beckman, and I have worked really hard with Cannon. We will never give up hope that he will TALK. A huge thank you to Dada, who feeds and gets the twins ready for Mum and Cannon by the time we come back and then works a full workday. I love that man!

After speech Cannon and I are headed to his preschool. Cannon did not even see me leave because he was so happy. Cannon attended one day before and he did okay, but now that he is feeling so much better we thought we would try another day. Cannon will go two mornings a week beginning in August when he turns three.

I confess, like I often do, I cried in the car as I left. But good tears... the tears that all mothers should have. Tears that my baby boy is happy, he has hair, eyebrows, eyelashes, an appetite, a smile on his face... all the joys every mother should see.

Leaving Cannon knowing he was happy... well, tears.

Tears... First Word
Written Apr 7, 2014 7:38am

We left speech therapy and I stopped to get gas before going to the hospital. As I was filling up, I heard the word, "Mum." Of course, I thought that I had dreamt I would hear that word for so long that I didn't believe my ears. So, I popped my head in the car and said to Cannon, "Mum?" He responded, "Mum, Mum, Mum, Mum..."

Yes, I am sobbing like a baby. Tears of joy!!!! We have been working so hard and everyone knows... winners never quit and quitters never win.

Cannonball will never quit...

I am on a pink cloud now and my tears won't stop. I think I'm going soft in my old age.

" Cannonball will never quit..."

Clear Scans... Almost NED (No Evidence of Disease)
Written Apr 9, 2014 5:44pm

Hooray for prayer warriors and modern medicine.

The scans showed no evidence of any cancer. Hit me!! High five!!

I'm doing my happy dance...

Tomorrow we will test urine, which to-date has still shown disease. Next week we will get the results from that test.

We are so very close to being able to say it... NED. Next week I believe we will say it!!

I'm ever grateful to everyone who prays and thinks about my baby!

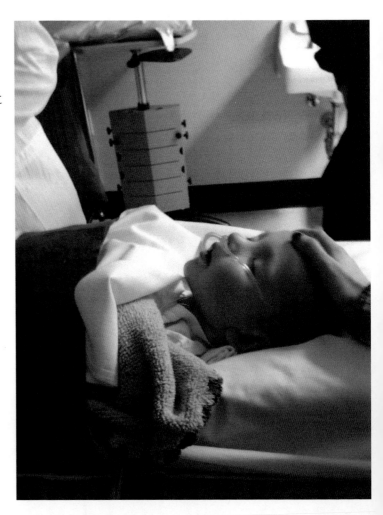

Dreaming Big
Written Apr 12, 2014 2:22pm

I am really trying to not think about Cannon being admitted tomorrow. Life has felt so normal lately it's hard to think about getting back in the ring with cancer. But I know this: cancer doesn't give up. One tiny cell, invisible to the eye, can turn into death for a child, so we can't give up and we can't stop.

Some would ask, "Why do you keep going?"

This is a marathon...

You don't stop at mile twenty-five and say, "Good job, I feel like I did well."

No, you keep going until the finish line.

> " You don't stop at mile twenty-five and say, 'Good job, I feel like I did well.'
>
> No, you keep going until the finish line."

That's what we're doing here... finishing the marathon!!!

Cannon will find out next week if there are any nb cancer cells in his urine. We are praying that there aren't, but either way it doesn't change our course of action. Cannon has three more rounds to go, two inpatient and one outpatient. Then he will finish the protocol but it's not the end of the road. Most likely, we will place Cannon on a trial drug called DFMO. We will travel to Michigan every three months for two years to participate in the trial (including taking scans and medications) and we will have monthly visits to our local hospital for bloodwork, etc.

The road for treatment is a long one. But I am thankful for the fact there is a protocol. Some cancers don't have one and doctors don't know what to do. Some parents are told their child has six months to a year to live. Cannon has a protocol and a chance of beating this, and we're taking that chance and we're running with it... all the way to the finish line.

See you all at the finish line where, hopefully next week, Cannon will get to hold a piece of paper for the first time saying, "I'm one day cancer-free!" That's the dream... I'm dreaming BIG!!!!

One Year Ago Today It All Began
Written Apr 14, 2014 2:57pm

This day (Monday) last year, Cannon started limping. We had been playing by the pool and he fell on the side of the pool. I thought maybe he had hurt his leg. Monday night, I put him to bed and had a pit in my stomach. I was thirty-seven weeks pregnant with our twins at that point, so I was a bit of a wreck and tried to let it go. I didn't sleep, I knew something wasn't right.

The next morning, Michael brought Cannon downstairs and he was limping so bad...

I can honestly remember it like it was yesterday. It makes me sick to my stomach to think about this week a year ago. Horrid, like a scary movie that never ends.

How blessed we are today as I lay in bed with Cannon and he is still fighting the beast. Some parents aren't where we are a year later. Some parents have already buried their angels. I get to cuddle mine as life-saving drugs pump into his veins for the next week.

What would be my wish? That this very week, a year from now, I can say my son is cancer-free. I am praying so hard for that. Is it too much to ask for? No. It's the only thing to ask for.

The Calm Before The Storm
Written Apr 16, 2014 9:57am

This day last year, Cannon and I stayed home. He wasn't able to walk anymore. Being heavily pregnant never stopped me (thirty-seven weeks with twins). I took Cannon everywhere, even Disney. People looked at me like I was crazy. I didn't care, I was determined to enjoy every last minute I had with just me and my buddy Cannonball. I knew life would be forever changed, I just didn't quite know how. I was determined - no nanny, just me - I could do this, right? I had a lot of plans for my three boys and myself. I still do, just a little later than I initially planned.

Michael was out of town. I called and told him Cannon wasn't able to walk and kept crawling. Michael told me something I'm ever grateful for. He said, "Push, Babe, push. If you believe something is wrong, then call the doctors back."

After I got off the phone with Michael, the doctor actually called me and asked how his leg was doing. I said, "Worse." The doctor told me to Google an orthopedic doctor and get an appointment.

I did exactly that. The next day (Thursday) we had our appointment.

We were at the ortho doctor's office almost all day. They did an X-ray. I was so pregnant they wouldn't let me go in and Cannon screamed and cried most of the day. Getting an X-ray alone at a year-and-a-half... yikes.

I am a hands-on mum. I asked to see the X-ray. It was so awful looking around his knees and lower leg. The doctor said it looked like a bacterial infection. We did another X-ray and Cannon was just traumatized by that point.

When I saw the X-ray, I knew something really bad was happening.

The doctor called for a CT scan tomorrow, stat, at Arnold Palmer Hospital for Children (APHC).

That night (Thursday), Michael got home from travel and he was just so upset. I said to him, "I hope it's not a tumor." Weird, right? Of course this upset him and he got upset with me for even suggesting it. I told him I knew something bad was happening and he didn't want to hear it... or believe it, I should say.

Friday, off we went to our first CT scan, experiencing what, at the time, was awful: starving our one and a half-year-old for the first time and watching him be put under.

By the time it was all done it was 5pm. The nurse said, "The doctor is coming to see you."

The doctor walked in and said, "It's osteomyelitis, an infection on the bone, and we're doing surgery." I looked at him and was like, "When?" OMG, my baby is having surgery? What? No... No... It was truly awful. Michael was so upset. Cannon was upset. I was, well, pregnant (that's all I need to say).

So, we went up to surgery. I called my family and told them to pray for Cannon.

It's really hard to type this through my tears, so I really do pray hard that people get something from this... hope... awareness. I just hope it does something for just one person today. I know I get so much from reading positive comments and prayers. I just hope I give that back.

We were waiting in surgery. I signed all the documents. Everyone was in scrubs. Remember, Cannon still hadn't eaten since the night before and it was now 6pm.

I am a very good people reader. I kept my ear and eyes on the surgeon the whole time. His body language changed. He made some calls. He said to a doctor on the phone, "These labs don't look right, his bloodwork isn't tying in. Could you have a look?"

The surgeon came over and said, "I don't want to freak you out but I just want a second opinion. The bloodwork isn't what I thought it would be and I just want to make sure we're not dealing with tumors or something else here. I don't think we are, but I want to double check. We will do the surgery tomorrow at 7am, but I want some consults for Cannon from oncology (that word gives me horrible goosebumps) and from some other teams."

I knew it in that moment... it was game over.

I knew it had been tumors... I just had a sense about it.

Michael went home to get a bag and explain to Olivia what was happening.

Friday... that night was the longest night ever. We did every test known to man. All night Cannon cried, test after test after test.

I recall like it was yesterday, the oncologist, Dr. Giusti, coming in our room and saying, "Look at that handsome boy... nothing wrong with him. Can I press his tummy?" Cannon sat on his lap. Dr. Giusti pressed his tummy and then he said, "Okay, well, I'm going to order some tests."

By 9pm the nurse came in and said, "Dr. Giusti wants to call your room." I felt like I was about to vomit. Why was the oncologist calling our room? No...

I picked up...

He said, "I don't think Cannon has a bone infection. I think he has neuroblastoma." I felt fuzzy-headed. I said, "What's that?" He said, "It's tumors." At that point, I could hardly breathe. I asked if I could pass the phone to Michael. I gave the phone to Michael and Googled "neuroblastoma". The results showed it was cancer. I got back on the phone and I said, "It's cancer?" He said, "Yes. I will come see you tomorrow morning to confirm."

I ran out of the room... I couldn't breathe... I had never had that feeling before... my chest was caving in... I was bawling... I could hardly breathe.

Michael was so brave. He said, "Babe, we don't know for sure. We will know tomorrow."

That was the only time I have bawled and fallen to the ground since Cannon was diagnosed.

Of course, I researched all night about neuroblastoma. I prayed all night, "Please not stage four." The statistics were so bad.

Dr. Giusti walked into our room at 6am.

He sat down and said, "So, it is neuroblastoma."

"What stage?" I asked.

"It's bad. It's stage four. It's all over his legs, under his arms and there's a huge tumor all over his abdomen. It's actually pushing his organs to the side it's so big. He has a battle on his hands."

I responded with a rhetorical question, "Yes, but he will survive? I mean, he won't die?"

"Fifty-fifty," Dr. Giusti said.

Looking back, I feel so bad for Dr. Giusti. Here was this man in his seventies telling a heavily pregnant woman her son could die. Can you imagine having that job? I praise these doctors so much. It's not a job I could do daily... and they're so dedicated. I'm ever grateful they sacrifice their lives for others.

Not cancer-Free... A People Pleaser No More

Written Apr 17, 2014 7:10am

So, we don't get to hold the sign up saying "cancer-free" just yet, but stay positive people. It's coming, I just know it is. I am not disappointed. Instead, I'm ever more determined.

Cannon is so close...

The urine numbers are shrinking and I'm positive that after this round of antibodies, Cannon will be officially NED. But not today... and that's okay.

When I came into this cancer world heavily pregnant with twins and as a new mum, it was safe to say people would call me a "people pleaser". I enjoyed making people happy, I still do. I was the person who, if I ordered coffee with no sugar and it came with sugar (even though I hate sugar in my coffee), I drank it because I didn't want to upset or inconvenience the server or cause any issues. Please don't think I was a pushover... I wasn't. I just liked everyone to be happy, and if people were unhappy, I was unhappy, so I kept the peace... always.

The cancer world changes you. No matter how hard you try not to, you change.

This world is not for the timorous. And as for people pleasers like me? Well, you realize it's a life or death situation you're in and REALLY, there is no room for people pleasing.

During the last round of antibodies I got into it with one of the doctors. I fought so hard for Cannon to receive them and even though they told me they strongly suggested we stop, I knew he needed them. I knew they would save him... and they are. The doctor and I were at it for over an hour (by "at it", I mean I felt like I was in court arguing for my client, just this time my client was my son).

If you would have told me a year ago I would strongly disagree with a doctor and tell that doctor to his face... me? The people pleaser? I would have said, "No way." Today, it's life or death, there is no room for people pleasing. Cannon needs me to suck it up and DO, and trust me, today I DO.

I am still extremely polite, no curse words are needed or necessary in my opinion. I can be articulate and passionate yet to the point, and that's the goal today.

I know as we enter next week, where we do the IL2 and the antibody, I will face the challenges again... and I'm ready. What is worth fighting for more than your own child? Nothing I can think of.

Cancer changes your child...

It also changes you...

And if you're lucky, you learn some REALLY valuable lessons along the road.

April 19, 2014, A Year Since Diagnosis
Written Apr 20, 2014 3:34pm

My heart is heavy as I write this post. Forgive me if I seem down, sad or pessimistic. I truly am trying to stay positive and I know my son NEEDS to go to ICU tonight if he is to be here April 19, 2015.

Yesterday marked one year exactly since it was confirmed...

"Your son has stage four neuroblastoma."

"Will he die?"

"He has a battle ahead of him... a long one. It's fifty-fifty."

It may sound strange, but Michael and I went on a date night last night to celebrate.

What are we celebrating?

We are celebrating the fact that our son is still fighting a year after he was diagnosed. So many kids die in the first year of this awful fight. Cannon is a blessed boy. He is alive and fighting... a gift.

I cherish every second with Cannon. I look at him so often and he smiles. He is always smiling, such a happy boy. Even when he is weak he is smiling. I wonder if these are my last days with him. I wonder if he will get to be with our family for all of his childhood, or will I bury him soon? Awful thoughts... an awful place to take your mind. Gut-wrenching. Sadly, sometimes my mind goes places no mother's mind should go. The truth? The honest truth? How do I live without my firstborn? How could I? I don't remember the last day my mind didn't go there, if even for just a moment.

Today, Cannon is so weak and has been since Friday. He is so pale, he is in real need of blood and thankfully, he will receive some tonight. Thank you to all of Cannon's faithful blood donors and the hundreds of others who give. It chokes me up because without them, Cannon would not be alive. I need people to know blood and platelet donations save the lives of kids like Cannon. Please don't ever stop donating... ever. Cannonball and all the kids with cancer need your donations, and from the bottom of my heart I'm ever grateful. For without you, I wouldn't have my baby by my side.

Tonight, AGAIN, Michael will take Cannon to fight the beast. He will go straight to the ICU where Cannon's life will be saved by the blood which is waiting for him. Then an IV will be placed and tomorrow we will begin the hardest round of antibodies, where two drugs rampage my son's thirty pound tiny body. I will watch, before my very eyes, my son go from smiling to crying and drugged up with morphine.

It never gets easier. I am not being pessimistic, just honest. My stomach aches for Cannon and my heart is crushed as I don't want to see him in pain, crying, struggling to breathe. It's so sad to watch... so hard.

BUT... mentally I must prepare. My dad used to tell me I would win the race only if I mentally believed I would win the race. I believe Cannon will win the race, but I have to mentally prepare to watch the horror that will be unveiled tomorrow. That's not a negative comment, it's a realistic one.

Being Strong: Next Round Of Antibody Therapy
Written Apr 22, 2014 10:02am

I find myself in the hospital chapel daily. I don't realize I'm going there until I am in it and praying on my knees to God to intervene and save my son, save all these kids. They deserve to experience college, get married, have babies. Yet the average age of a kid that dies with cancer is eight. Many are much younger.

In the chapel, I can be vulnerable and that's a nice feeling. Everywhere else I can't. Cannon can't see me cry, he must know I am strong and this doesn't hurt me. Why? I recall an incredible boy with bone cancer who once told me, "The hardest part of having cancer is watching my parents in pain, seeing my Mum cry." So from that very day I made it my mission to not make this any harder on Cannon than it needs to be.

We just started day two of this round of antibodies. Cannon was in need of a catheter last night and today. We got 800 mls of urine from him. He is retaining so much fluid and now his lungs are getting wet. It's a challenge battling pain with respiratory issues. My heart aches for Cannon, my husband Michael and my sister, as I see them all sad. When Cannon is sad, they are sad. When Cannon is happy, they are carefree, happy spirits. Cancer weighs heavy on everyone in a family. My mother calls me every day from Scotland asking how he is doing. She has to watch both her grandson and me in pain, can you imagine? Awful.

Prayers We Can Get Out Today: Antibody Therapy
Written Apr 25, 2014 9:33am

Cannon is having bad hives. It's amazing to look at the change in him. Emotionally, it's a roller coaster ride because he comes in happy and appearing healthy, and he leaves unwell and so sick.

We may not get out tonight. We won't be done with the treatment until 6pm. If Cannon is able to urinate on his own, we can get out. We removed the cath yesterday to try and get him to urinate on his own, but we had to reinsert it. We will remove it again at 1pm. Please pray for Cannonball.

It's been a hard week, but Cannon keeps Cannonballing Kids' cancer. He can do this.

Home Finally
Written Apr 26, 2014 10:28am

We finally got home from the ER last night, however, they want us to go back to the ER today, and then on Monday we have the oncology clinic. We love you APHC, but we just wish we could have time together in our little haven and be as a family.

Cannon is just so not himself, a combination of being in a bed for a week and withdrawing from high doses of morphine, albeit less than before.

Cannon's body is getting tired and so is his mind. Last night he was beyond over being in the hospital and my heart bled for him. I don't ask why, I never have. I think the answer back would be, "Why not your child?" Instead, I try to fix it, change it, do anything to make it to mile twenty-six.

I know the next two years - including traveling to Michigan every three months for a one week stay (if we decide on the trial) - will be a challenge, but nothing can compare to being in the ICU and watching my child fight day after day for his life.

Cannon was up during the night with awful diarrhea, bless his heart. He just feels so unwell. Today Michael took him for a drive (one of his favorite activities) while I fed the twins breakfast. Fifteen minutes later, Michael was shouting for me to come to the garage door, where I saw Cannon standing there with diarrhea literally head-to-toe. Up his back, down his legs, on his stomach. I just kept telling him it was okay because he was so embarrassed. It made me feel so bad for him... he looked so sad and ashamed.

Cancer is tough. Cannon is tougher.

I believe he can beat this disease.

Ask Not For Lesser Burdens, But Broader Shoulders

Written Apr 27, 2014 3:45pm

Today I need strength. I am weary, worn down, emotional and anxious. Watching your child go from looking healthy and being happy to what I hold in my arms now is so exhausting. I truly can't imagine how my son feels. He is such a warrior to me. I am so the caregiver and not the patient.

As I type, Cannon just finished insanely crying. He is resting his head on me as we lie on the sofa and try to watch some movies.

He wants to eat, but feels sick.

He wants to play, but has no energy.

He wants to smile, but is too weary.

Cannon is withdrawing badly from the drugs. We've had this issue before, it's not pretty, but what is in the world of childhood cancer?

Cannon's nose runs, his head is sore from dehydration due to diarrhea every few hours, every bone in his body aches. He is weary and miserable.

Last night Michael and I were up the entire night with him. We slept for maybe two hours between us. It's hard when you have a 6am wakeup call with the twins who are full of love and energy. They truly do make me smile daily. I can't believe they're turning one in three days.

I never ask for lesser burdens, but for stronger shoulders. I truly do need more strength to get through these last few months. Just between us... I do pray for NO more burdens. That might be cheating, but it's our secret...

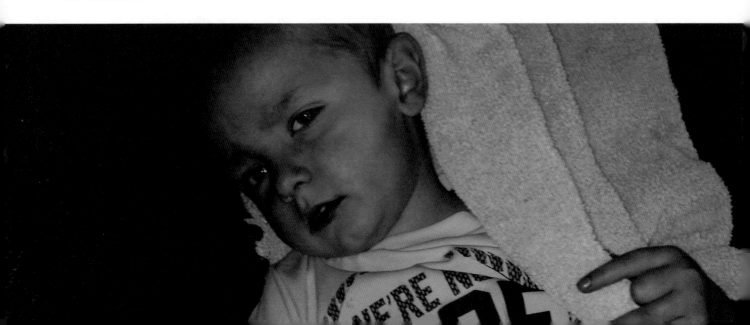

I Wish I Could Change Cannon's Journey

Written Apr 29, 2014 1:00pm

My heart bleeds for Cannon... what he has endured, does endure, and will endure.

Our childhood is the time when you sleep late, eat bad food and don't gain weight, play all day, don't work, have no bills. It's a time in our lives we all should truly appreciate more. No stress, just fun.

At a year and a half, Cannon's fun-loving, playful days have ended. He will be three in August and has spent half of his life fighting a beast of a cancer, one that takes more kids than any other, and one that wants to take my son.

Cannon should be talking, running, jumping off of things. He should not be in the ICU fighting for his life.

I ache for him. It's physically painful. My heart hurts, my chest is always tight and I feel the weight of the world is on my shoulders... over and over the feeling of being run over by a train.

Cannon and I were up at 3am and the twins awoke from hearing Cannon crying. It's heartbreaking to see him this way AGAIN, over and over and over AGAIN. He is anxious, not a feeling he should even know yet.

I am not giving up,

I never will.

I'm tired,

but, more than that,

Cannon is tired.

I feel this treatment is pushing him to his limits.

I know it has to in order for Cannon to stay alive.

But, it's beyond comprehension watching him suffer over and over again.

I think about how Cannon can't have kids and how it will pain him as an adult to not provide his wife the ability to carry a child. It's one of the reasons I so badly believe adoption is in our future; to show Cannon his parents loved their adopted child as much as him, and so he can love that way, too.

Please pray for Cannon to heal quickly. He is struggling and, as his mother, it is unbearable to watch.

Happy 1st Birthday Twin Boys

Written Apr 30, 2014 8:55am

On April 30, 2013, two beautiful boys were placed in my arms... six pounds, three ounces and six pounds, six ounces. They were perfect. They ARE perfect to me.

I know this day a year ago was awful, but today it is not. Today, I ran into their room singing "Happy Birthday", and singing ain't ma thing friends, so you know it's a good day. I want to celebrate the twins. They deserve to be celebrated. I carry so much guilt towards them for not being around like I should.

Cannon was diagnosed on April 19, 2013, just eleven days before the twins were born. I left him for the first time and walked across the street to the baby hospital to give birth to the twins. I left Cannon in ICU as he was doing chemo with his dad. He had already had two surgeries that week. A few nights before their birth I told my husband he needed to stay with Cannon. Cannon needed him way more than I did. So my mum came to the birth of the twins, which I know she loved. It was a very special moment for their grandmother to be in the room during the birth of her grandbabies.

I had so looked forward to the birth of the boys. Cancer ripped it from me, from my husband and from our family. Cancer will not steal the joy in my heart today.

May 7th 2014

384 DAYS

SINCE DIAGNOSIS

The average age of diagnosis of a child with cancer is 6 and the number of years of life lost to cancer for that child is 71. When children die of cancer, they are robbed of growing up, marrying, having children of their own, creating something beautiful the world has never seen, or even discovering a cure for cancer.

*Source: St. Baldrick's

New Saying: Happy Kids - Happy Life
Written May 7, 2014 4:28pm

I know the saying goes, "happy wife, happy life", but I've decided to change it: "Happy kids, happy parents, happy life."

When Cannon is happy, everything is different. The twins feel it, Olivia feels it, Auntie Nicole feels it and my marriage feels it. Life is just different.

It's hard to truly show in words what my heart feels today. Some examples of joy I have witnessed:

1. Cannon standing and going round and round in a circle.

2. Cannon running around a stand in the Disney Store and giggling over and over.

3. Cannon, for the first time since being diagnosed, truly playing in the splash pad. He even outplayed his brothers, who were pooped out before him.

The twins feel his energy and the lightness and joy in the hearts of Auntie Nicole and me, and it truly is a domino effect. Everyone is happier and life is easier... much easier.

Ten more sleeps to our inpatient stay, not that I'm counting. I'm trying to live in the moment. Next week, we will take urine and confirm what I believe is true - NED... no evidence of disease.

Also, Michael and I have decided to go to Michigan for the DFMO trial. May I add that nine kids are on this trial at Arnold Palmer Hospital for Children, and they aren't allowing any more kids to participate (it's not an easy explanation). I am not giving up hope of changing their minds and allowing us in the trial, but if my efforts fail then Michigan it is. Any lengths for our son!!! Any...

Go BIG Or Go HOME
Written May 9, 2014 4:16pm

Yesterday I had an interview with the local newspaper, the "Orlando Sentinel", as they are doing an article on Cannon for Mother's Day. One of the questions they asked me was, "It must be so difficult sharing your most intimate feelings and being vulnerable. What motivates you?" I told him I recalled the exact time and place when Michael and I discussed "Go BIG or go HOME."

" Cute bald kids smiling on TV is not the reality of kids' cancer. In fact... it's the exact reason (or one the reasons) there is a lack of funding; people think it's cute kids and they all survive! "

We were at Memorial Sloan Kettering Cancer Center in New York. Cannon lay before us after a thirteen hour surgery. He was on life support and I said to Michael, "Should we let the world see this?" Michael said, "I can't, it's too painful." I said, "That's exactly why we must." There and then everything changed. We said, "Go big or go home." It's all or nothing. Cute bald kids smiling on TV is NOT the reality of kids' cancer. IN FACT... it's the exact reason (or one the reasons) there is a lack of funding; people think it's cute kids and they all survive! They don't all survive and they're not all smiles and laughter - not even close. Sorry, I am getting to the point. You can see it's difficult for me not to get fired up when I start writing about this topic. Anyway, the truth is I write and blog about Cannon for many reasons, but the number one reason, and by far the most significant, is to raise awareness about kids' cancer.

Tomorrow Cannon will strut his stuff on the runway at a kids' cancer event run by the charity Runway to Hope, which was started by a local attorney and his wife. To-date, the charity has raised almost three million dollars for kids' cancer funding for our local hospitals. Cannon got to pick out clothes and will walk with a local celebrity. It will be such an amazing, fun event. Can't wait!

Time... Life Is What You Make Of It
Written May 12, 2014 8:18pm

I just returned from a date night with Michael since our usual Saturday date night was spent going to the Runway to Hope event this week, and Michael goes out of town tomorrow until Friday night for work. It got me thinking...

Time is our greatest, most valuable commodity. You can't ever recreate it and that makes it more valuable than anything. We get one chance at this life. Our time is our investment to life, the world and to ourselves.

This past year since Cannon was diagnosed, time has become MORE valuable to me than ever. I've had to make changes.

I feel more than ever that I must use my time wisely with PURPOSE and without distractions. Almost everything I do is with PURPOSE and passion. Not everything, but a lot. Everything in moderation, right? ;)

For example, in a practical sense, I have even started setting my phone in my bathroom, away from me, so I can focus on my children. If you know me, that's quite a change. I don't need to be on social media or calls to Scotland for hours when my kids are awake and want their Mumma-Bear. I can use naptime or bedtime to catch up with people or check social media. Easier said than done, but entirely possible. I'm a work in progress but I'm getting there.

I believe that in order to reach the full potential of our Cannonball Kids' cancer Foundation – to increase funding for more than four percent, educate to eradicate and promote the need for blood drives - I must be focused and disciplined. Being a stay-at-home mum since Cannon was diagnosed and having three kids under three with no nanny, I find that in order to get anything done I need sticky notes, phone alarms and calendars, and I need to be motivated during naps and after the kids go to bed. It's easy to just sit on the sofa when it's naptime and pass out and sometimes, trust me, I do. But I want Cannonball Kids' cancer (CKc) to help all of the other teams out there fighting kids' cancer and that takes teamwork and above all, being disciplined and motivated.

I started by making small changes: Not allowing people to just drop in at my house, planning my week on a Sunday night including time with other mothers, hospital appointments, CKc meetings, date night, a day out with the boys, grocery day, etc., and writing notes the night before on what I want to achieve the next day. Not much in my life is impromptu anymore, and for me, my family and our situation with Cannon, it's working. I feel motivated and purposeful today. That doesn't mean I will tomorrow, but I am today.

I believe that what has happened with Cannon has truly toughened me up. I used to say to Michael, "I don't want to hurt their feelings." Michael would say, "So you hurt yourself?" It's true. Wasting time on unproductive things or with negative people that aren't like-minded or better-minded is only hurting oneself.

Today I consider every moment of time valuable, not because I am any better or worse than you, not because I'm less or more important, but because I have learned the hard way that life can change forever in an instant. That life can end in an instant. That life is what YOU make it!!! No one can do it for you. I try more than ever to enjoy every second with my kids and husband. Even when I'm totally exhausted I try to be grateful, for I know it could be taken from me and from our family at any moment.

Delayed Response
Written May 14, 2014 6:36pm

First and most important, Cannon is on fire. He truly is a "ten" on the happy scale. He is smiling all day, eating (not the food I want, but eating nonetheless – Mumma-Bear can't have it all) and playing. He truly has come so far.

This morning we did speech for the first time in four weeks and it was amazing. He ran in all happy and did wonderful. To-date, the only word he says is "Mum", but I will never give up and I will try to get him to talk with all I have.

Sunday we will be admitted to the hospital for what WILL be (I'm believing) Cannon's last inpatient stay in the ICU or hospital EVER!!

It's strange, I have felt so strong this entire year. Like a bull in a China shop, nothing has stood in my way to get Cannon what he has needed. A strength I NEVER knew I had, and I don't say this because I wasn't a strong person before, I say it because I always used to say, "No matter what, I could never deal with losing my child or a sick child."

The point is, you don't realize you can handle things until they are thrown your way. I feel like we were walking in the rain this time last year and the sun will soon shine brightly on our baby and our lives.

Today Is A Very Big Day
Written May 17, 2014 9:25am

Cannon and I are just about to go to the hospital for his urine test. This test will confirm if Cannon has any neuroblastoma left in his body. I have waited so long and I yearn to hear those three magic words...

No Evidence of Disease...

NED...

Please pray that Cannon is finally, after fourteen months, cancer-free.

Mumma-Bear is a nervous wreck.

Normalcy... Thirteen Months Since Diagnosis
Written May 17, 2014 9:28am

This past week felt like an "almost" normal week. Cannon has been on no medications (a real rarity) and as a result, we got to not only witness but enjoy the REAL Cannonball... smiles, hugs, kisses, giggles and dancing in circles galore.

It's been food for Mumma-Bear's aching soul.

BRAG spoiler: Cannonball finally went over his weight at diagnosis (thirty pounds at twenty months old). Cannon now weighs... wait for it... thirty-three pounds, four ounces. I am so proud of him!!!

Worst Day In A Long Time: Another Round Of Antibody Therapy
Written May 19, 2014 5:33pm

The sound of my twin baby boys talking to each other early this morning as I packed my bag for my hospital stay with Cannon - the giggles, the coo sounds, the sound of toys being played with over the monitor - set me off. I wouldn't... I won't get to hear that noise for three days. Today I am in the ICU with Cannon until Michael returns on Wednesday from work travel.

I can't lie, today has been incredibly soul destroying. It is 6pm and since 11am, Cannon has slept and rested only thirty minutes the entire day. It has been the worst day in a very long time. We came in last night thinking this round would be easy since it was only the antibody, not the antibody and the IL2. But, that's cancer. You put down your defenses for a moment and, bam, it's all guns blazing. I feel like I'm in a sinking ship and I have no life vest for Cannon. The pain and misery he has endured today is like nothing I've seen in a long time. You'd think I would have built up some tolerance for seeing the pain in my son's eyes as three others and I hold him down to put in a cath or an IV. Well, I haven't! It's like a new experience, each time more painful than the time before. I wish I could tell you it was easier, less painful...

The reality...

You can't...

You won't...

Ever...

Get used to seeing your child in pain and sick!! Period.

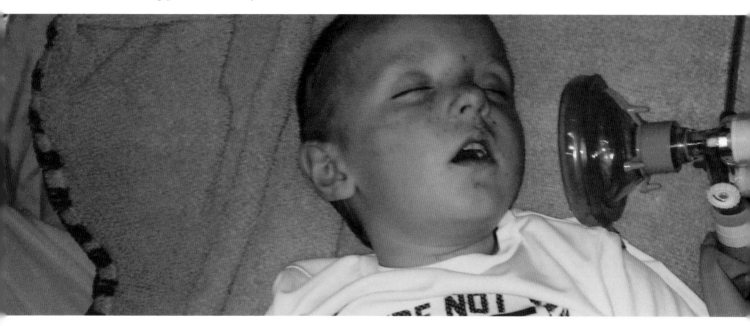

NO Evidence Of Disease... cancer-Free!
Written May 20, 2014 12:37pm

"cancer-Free!"

No Evidence of Disease

Ahhhhhhhhhhhh!!!!

Finally!!!!

Cannon has worked so hard for this day...

I confess, I cried when Dr. Susan Kelly showed me the
results from his last urine test and then today's results.
It wasn't pretty but it couldn't be held back. A rush of
emotions flew through my body.

Cannon's levels are now 3.8 and 6.2 (below thirteen is normal). When he was diagnosed they were 300. We know we still have two years of outpatient treatments but that's our insurance policy for what we already know. Cannon has no evidence of any disease in his body.

Today, May 20, 2014, is a day I will never ever forget!! Ever!!!

I am not sure how to express in words the feeling in my heart and soul. The truck that was pushing me against the wall over and over yesterday has released me from its grip, and finally the pressure from my chest is lessening. My sister brought the twins to see me and I got to share the amazing news with her and the boys.

Cannon has slept almost all day since he didn't sleep last night. I should probably try and rest but I am just so happy that everything we have worked so hard for is paying off. Cannon did this; no one else can take that from him. We just helped him along the way, but Cannon did this. He went through a thirteen hour surgery, he was taken to near death in transplant... he did it all. I am so proud of that kid I get to call my son. Michael and I are just so happy!! I can't wait to hug my husband and really celebrate.

We're Not Here To Lose
Written May 21, 2014 8:11am

What a difference a few days in the ICU makes to my son.

The happiness is sucked from him... literally.

Cannon has been beyond agitated this round. He is OVER it!! I have never seen him so agitated and mad for such a prolonged period of time. That is so not his character, but when pushed...

We're not here to LOSE!!!

So what's next for Cannonball?

Now it's the preventative, NOT curative stage!! It feels nice to think that we are in the preventative stage now.

Prevention of the "R" word... Relapse.

After this round is complete, we will have two more outpatient rounds and then the scans and tests to complete the protocol, all of which should be complete by the third week in July. Then no time to waste - off to Michigan. We must start the DFMO two-year trial within thirty days of completing the Children's Oncology Group (COG) protocol we are on now. So Cannon will start August 2014 and complete August

2016. Cannon will be five years old then. He was diagnosed at twenty months. Thankful for the fight!!!!

After we're done with protocol in July, we will do monthly visits to APHC for bloodwork, scans, etc. for two years. Then every three months we will stay in Michigan for about a week, for scans and checks, etc. Cannon will take, I believe, four capsules twice daily for two years. Side effects are more hearing loss but it's temporary while on the drugs. Aside from that, Cannon should be able to have a great, happy life and feel good.

The Greater The Difficulty, The Greater The Glory... Last Antibody Therapy EVER
Written May 22, 2014 2:44pm

" The greater the difficulty, the greater the glory."

~ Marcus T. Cicero

Not. A. Truer. Statement. Exists. For. Today.

You know, when you become a mother you imagine many things - planning birthday parties, making scavenger hunts, building projects. I can't say I ever imagined planning an end of chemo/treatment party but that is what we did today. We celebrated the last bag of antibodies our son will ever endure.

Continue The Fight - Blog By Dad, Michael Wiggins
Written May 23, 2014 8:48am

Melissa and I have seen it all, and I nearly shake in anger and my eyes well up when I see my son suffering, yet again, from an IV needle that has come out and has to be replaced, or his nausea from receiving multiple medications, or his eyes rolling back from so much morphine to shut off some of the pain, or when I contemplate the fact that he has not eaten a single crumb since Sunday night because he feels too ill to do so, or I see him stumble on his feet because his legs have no strength after lying in bed listlessly for days.

THIS is the world of kids' cancer. This is it. It's not kids with bald heads holding balloons, a stuffed animal or toy and smiling. It's just not, and perhaps the reason why kids' cancer gets so little attention in our world is because most would like to have it painted this way.

Never forget, every day parents bury children lost to cancer. Every day when you are getting ready for work, your day, school or an adventure, there are others also dressing and preparing, but to attend the funeral of their child, the average age of eight... dead and gone forever and so unjustly and, in our opinion, needlessly. It is wrong. Please help Melissa and me continue this fight.

Ten Days cancer-Free
Written May 30, 2014 8:51pm

Celebrating ten days cancer-free...

We went to a local farm today and the boys had a blast.

Cannon is still very agitated with his medications and has severe mood swings. When he isn't on any meds he truly is, well, very different.

I have always been the one who administers Cannon's shots (jags, to my UK friends) and it tears me up to say this, but last night I gave Cannon the last ever home health shot I will EVER have to give, but more important, Cannon had his last shot. He is the one who truly suffers daily, not me. I didn't get a shot in my legs daily, he did. So I'm beyond thankful that Cannon doesn't need to endure any more pain in his muscles and joints via the shots.

June 7th 2014

415 DAYS

SINCE DIAGNOSIS

The number of diagnosed cases of children's cancer has not declined in 20 years. The incidence rate of cancer occurring in our children has risen 29% over that time period. That means today more kids are being diagnosed with cancer per 100 children than were being diagnosed as of 1990.

*Source: Cancer.gov

Nothing Is Impossible
Written Jun 7, 2014 1:33pm

I was listening this morning to a famous baseball player, Michael Milken, who started a charity for prostate cancer, and the truly incredible advancements his foundation has made. It made me tear up. I am ever grateful to those who devote their lives to charity. It can be done! It is not impossible! HE motivated me.

I am motivated beyond my own comprehension. I believe in our Team: you guys!!! I believe we can make a difference. Kids shouldn't suffer like we (and you) saw Cannon suffer, or worse... DIE!!

"Nothing is impossible, the word itself says I'm Possible."

~Audrey Hepburn

The average age of a man diagnosed with prostate cancer is seventy. The average age of a kid that DIES from cancer is eight. The number of years lost for kids is insane!
It is possible! It can be done! Prostate cancer advancements prove my point! I am so happy these advancements in prostate cancer have been made. Help me! Help these kids! Let's model prostate cancer and make the same changes for kids.

"Nothing is impossible, the word itself says I'M POSSIBLE." ~ Audrey Hepburn

In 1975, women with breast cancer had a fifty-five percent chance of survival. Now, the survival rate is ninety percent. So aside from kids' leukemia, which has a high rate of survival at ninety percent, kids' cancer is where breast cancer was forty years ago. If it's possible for prostate and breast cancer to move forward like they have with:

· Early detection
· Education
· Fundraising

(which are all in our mission at Cannonball Kids' cancer), then WE CAN DO THIS!!!!

It's NOT All Smiles And Balloons

Written Jun 26, 2014 6:30am

Cannon is cancer-free, shouldn't it be all smiles and balloons like we see on the TV?

That is such a huge misconception...

What does thirty-six days cancer-free REALLY look like?

Cannon woke up at 1am screaming.

It looks like this: anxiety attacks.

Despite the fact that Cannon is considered "NED" (no evidence of disease), the sheer misery of cancer still invades our lives; every aspect of our lives.

Cannon, at two years of age, takes four large capsules a day. They make him anxious and scared and give him mood swings. He is two! The medication he is getting is for adolescents and adults. He is two!! Why? Because the pharmaceutical companies don't make drugs for children, and the government is only giving us less than four percent of the funding pie to be divided amongst more than 100 types of kids' cancers.

It looks like clinic appointments where a medicine is pumped into Cannon's veins through a port in his chest for forty-five minutes and he has diarrhea explosions all over him, down his legs, not once, but twice.

It's placing pee bags over his penis and waiting for hours for him to urinate.

It looks like being sedated and placed on his stomach while holes are drilled into his back to take a sample of his bone marrow.

It looks like toxic medicine being pumped into him for three days in a row so he can be sedated again for two days in a row and given two full body scans.

After that's all done, he is off to Michigan to get on yet another trial, which will mean two years of traveling to Michigan, not to mention taking eight capsules a day!

Why?

Well, like we were told on day one, the cancer Cannon has kills more kids than any other form of kids' cancer.

Why?

Because it comes back. So even though we don't see any cancer on Cannon's scans, there's a pretty good chance it is still there, and if it comes back, there is no cure and you would just be buying time.

I'm sorry, WHAT?!

So chemo, surgeries, stem cell transplant, radiation, six months of antibody therapy, two years of DFMO and it will PROBABLY come back? I don't understand!

Cannon didn't get back to sleep until around 4am. He cried, needed comforting and was anxious beyond what any two year-old should ever know.

So no, cancer-free ISN'T all smiles and balloons.

It's living in three month segments waiting for the next scan.
It's daily medications.
It's sleepless nights with anxiety.
It's sore stomachs from the medicines.
It's hearing aids.
It's occupational therapy.
It's speech.
It's educational physiologists.
It's physical therapy.
It's eating issues.
It's diarrhea.
It's weakness.

It's NOT all smiles and balloons.

Cannon is impacted for the rest of his life. Someday I have to tell him he can't have children. Someday he has to tell his partner that!

It's been said before, the treatments these kids endure are barbaric, dated and not in line with other treatments for adult cancers. If you don't agree with that statement, head to your local hospital and shadow a child life expert and watch the misery that is in the playroom of kids with cancer.

Cancer!

It has changed OUR family forever!!

The treatments he endures are dated and barbaric! That's right, I said the word! And it's true!

Someone said yesterday that we don't use computers that are fifty, forty, or thirty years old, yet we use dated treatments on the greatest gifts of our lives - our children, our grandchildren.

It's not right, fair or just!

It has to change!

One mad Mumma-Bear!!!

July 2nd 2014

440 DAYS

SINCE DIAGNOSIS

One in 330 children will be diagnosed with
cancer by the time they are 20 years old.

*Source: Alex's Lemonade Stand

Cast A Stone Across Waters To Create Many Ripples
Written Jul 2, 2014 1:49pm

Where to begin...

So much is happening so fast. It is a ride I never imagined I would get on but one I know I will never get off.

I love this quote someone sent to me:

"I alone cannot change the world, but I can cast a stone across waters to create many ripples." ~ Mother Teresa

The Foundation: Cannonball Kids' cancer, founded June 10, 2014, was created not only by Michael and me but by all of you. I truly believe in the quote above by Mother Teresa. There is nothing that has been achieved so far that is by Michael and me alone – nothing. It has been teamwork all the way and now that team is growing at an exponential speed.

I want everyone to know that although this isn't a "real" job in the sense that my husband and I are not compensated monetarily, I take my position within the Board and the Foundation VERY seriously. I have never been more dedicated to anything in my life. I spend hours daily working towards a successful movement to eradicate pediatric cancer through education. "Educate to Eradicate."

I fully believe we have two choices with our words:
1. We can use them to complain, or
2. We can use them to change our situation.

I choose CHANGE. What use is it to sit around and cry over spilled milk? My son had cancer (forty-one days cancer-free, people!). He may even get it again or get another secondary cancer. Instead, why not share the experience and make good of it? Make those ripples in the water, ripples of good, ripples of hope, ripples of faith, RIPPLES OF EDUCATION. We at Cannonball Kids' cancer believe in our hearts that if we educate more people, things CAN and WILL change!

Made in the USA
Charleston, SC
11 February 2017